THE POWERS OF THE WORD

PRINCIPAL WORKS OF RENÉ DAUMAL

Le Contre-ciel (poems), 1936.
La Grande beuverie (novel), 1938.
Le Mont Analogue (novel), 1952.
Lettres à ses amis, I (correspondence), 1959.
Bharata (essays), 1970.
L'Evidence absurde: essais et notes, I (1926-1934), 1972.
Les Pouvoirs de la parole: essais et notes, II (1935-1943), 1972.
Le Grand Jeu (facsimile), 1977.

In English Translation

Mount Analogue, translated by Roger Shattuck
A Night of Serious Drinking, translated by David Coward
and E.A. Lovatt
Rasa, or Knowledge of the Self, translated by
Louise Landes Levi
Selected poems in *The Poetry of Surrealism* and *The Random House Book of Twentieth-Century French Poetry.*

René Daumal

THE
POWERS
OF THE
WORD

Selected Essays and Notes
1927-1943

Edited and translated
with an Introduction
by
MARK POLIZZOTTI

CITY LIGHTS BOOKS
San Francisco

Selections from *L'Evidence absurde: essais et notes, I (1926-1934)* by
René Daumal copyright © 1972 by Editions Gallimard. Selections
from *Les Pouvoirs de la parole: essais et notes, II (1935-1943)* by René
Daumal copyright © 1972 by Editions Gallimard.
Translation and Introduction copyright © 1991 by Mark Polizzotti
First published by City Lights Books in 1991.
Cover photograph: René Daumal at around age 15, experimenting
with "paroptic vision" at the home of his teacher, René Maublanc.
(Photo: René Maublanc)
Cover design: John Miller / Big Fish Books

Library of Congress Cataloging-in-Publication Data

Daumal, René, 1908-1944.
    [Essais et notes: English. Selections]
    The powers of the word : [selected essays and
notes] / by René Daumal ; translated from the French
by Mark Polizzotti.
    p.   cm.
    Translation of selections from L'évidence absurde
and Les pouvoirs de la parole, which were published
under the collective title, Essais et notes.
    Includes bibliographical references.
    IBSN 0-87286-259-3 ; $12.95
    1. Daumal, René, 1908-1944 –Translations into
English. I. Title. PQ2607.A86A26 1991
PQ2607.A86A26   1991
844'.912--dc20
                                      91-10331
                                        CIP

City Lights Books are available to bookstores through our primary
distributor: Subterranean Company, P.O. Box 168, 265 S. 5th Street,
Monroe, Oregon 97456. (503) 847-5274. Our books are also available
through library jobbers and regional distributors. For personal
orders and catalogs, please write to City Lights Books, 261
Columbus Avenue, San Francisco, California 94133.

CITY LIGHTS BOOKS are edited by Lawrence Ferlinghetti and
Nancy J. Peters and published at the City Lights Bookstore,
261 Columbus Avenue, San Francisco, California 94133

TABLE OF CONTENTS

THE POWERS OF THE WORD:
SELECTED ESSAYS AND NOTES
1927-1943

RENE DAUMAL

Like virtually all major thinkers, René Daumal was both profoundly of his time and far removed from it. And as with many major thinkers, his work remained all but unknown until after his death. Overshadowed by the extravagance and self-promoting polemics of Surrealist-dominated French thought, Daumal's sober brilliance was not apt to attract the notoriety on which André Breton and company thrived. When in 1944 he succumbed to chronic ill-health, the war's hardships and his own unrelenting quest for knowledge, there was little to indicate that nearly twenty years of rigorous literary production and spiritual progress would ever be noticed by more than a handful of friends and collaborators. And yet Daumal and his group were the logical extension of what Surrealism had begun: they were at once enthusiastic and skeptical; orthodox and iconoclastic; and finally, resolutely independent of their predecessors.

Although a few of his writings saw the light of day during his lifetime, Daumal did not truly come into his own until the publication of *Mount Analogue*, nearly a decade after his death. It has since come to be regarded as a modern classic. A quantity of other works appeared in its wake, including writings on Hindu theater, a poorly-edited volume of letters, and the known balance of his poetry. The essays and notes, of which the present volume is a sampling, were not collected in book form until 1972; with few exceptions, this is their first appearance in English. A number of essays, letters, etc., remain unavailable to this day. In an age that treats the uncompromising search for self-knowledge as a luxury, we can almost wonder that any of these texts were published at all.[1]

1. In the course of these essays, the reader will notice an almost insistent repetition of images and examples—the sign, perhaps, of an author uncertain about *just how much* of his work will ever be read.

i

I have called these essays the work of a major thinker, and such a claim requires justification. To my mind, Daumal's unsparing lucidity; the vast range, depth and purpose of his erudition; the humor that never ceases to question all claims to "truth" or "knowledge"– particularly his own; his life-long efforts to make Poetry an expression of *lived* experience and to eradicate the empty "chatterings" that so-called poetry willingly accomodates (see "On the Attitude of Criticism With Respect to Poetry" and "Poetry Black, Poetry White," both exemplary in this regard); his confrontation of intense childhood fears and physical frailty to illuminate the great mystery of death – these alone would warrant him a place in any pantheon of letters. There is more.

But let us come full circle.

"Fear-of-death."

René Daumal was born on March 16, 1908, in Boulzicourt (Ardennes), France, a small working-class town not far from the Belgian border. His father, a local teacher, is described as a "convinced atheist with an austere and intransigent morality" committed to socialist-revolutionary ideals. From his grandfather, René inherits an interest in occult traditions. He will later write of his origins: "My race is an exquisite mixture of Mongoloid, Celtic, Germanic, Spanish and others which don't even have a name." A good if not brilliant student, he teaches himself to read at age four, and is later described by childhood friend Luc Périn as "curious about everything and a voracious reader. He loved biology and avidly collected beetles." During the war, René pursues his primary-school studies in a variety of locales, and briefly joins the Médrano circus as a clown. He later summarizes these years: "Paris. Bombardment. Cellars. Boom Boom, like at the Médrano circus where I try out my young talents."

At age six, Daumal experiences what will become a primary force behind his work: the fear of death. In "The Determining Memory" he relives the "horrible nights" spent "clawed in the stomach and held in a stranglehold by the dread of nothingness." And in an early poem he says:

> Somewhere in the night a mollusc is growing
> – but where does he get his flesh from?–
> he grows with the little pale balls
> in the pits of childish stomachs:

ii

these knots that inflate in the belly and beneath
   the ribcage,
   that people call "fear-of-death."

It is characteristic of Daumal's thought process that this fear of death should become a will to conquer it, to understand at all costs what lies *beyond* it, in the realm where verbal language is merely the first step toward experience, the outer door of mystery: "every day I read, on an iron gate near our house, the prophetic inscription: MORTAL DANGER."

Reims: Simplism, "experimental metaphysics" and "fundamental experience"

With the end of the war, René's studies are characterized by a diminishing respect for traditional forms of education. His readings include Victor Hugo, Jules Verne and books on the occult. In 1922 the Daumals move to Reims where René, now at the *lycée*, finds himself in class with Roger Vailland (later awarded the Prix Goncourt for his novel *The Law*), Robert Meyrat and Roger Gilbert-Lecomte. Two weeks late, solitary, the newcomer is described as being "expressionless, spare of gesture and word; he made one think of a Buddha." Lecomte quickly penetrates this impassive skin, discovers numerous affinities with the "new kid," and invites him to join their evening readings of the *poètes maudits*, among whom Lecomte includes himself. The four classmates soon constitute a kind of secret society, with its own codes and rites. They consider themselves "Angels" fallen to Earth, each with his own characteristics: Daumal is the exile, soft-spoken and patient, dreaming of paradises lost; Lecomte is the visionary, the vampire, friend to Satan and spectres; Vailland, the most "earth-bound" of the four, combats ingrained Catholic guilt (which will later give way to a self-styled libertinism and fervent Stalinism) and writes newspaper articles for pocket money; Meyrat is taciturn, mysterious and frightening. They name themselves collectively, as the "Simplist Brothers," and individually: Daumal is "Nathaniel" or "Phils" (son) to Lecomte's "Papa"; Lecomte will also go by the mock-aristocratic "Coco de Colchilde" and the vampire-tinged "Rog Jarl"; Vailland is "Dada" or, reflecting his more bourgeois mentality, "François"; Meyrat is simply "the Ghoul." They spend their days together, excluding practically all others, and seeing themselves as one and the same—four

iii

aspects of a single Angel. "I am not a solitary angel, oh Francois, since we are four," Daumal writes to Vailland in 1925. "But we four are the Simplist Archangel."

Who are the "Simplists"? In a letter dated 1926 to Maurice Henry, a future member of the group (later a well-known cartoonist), Daumal describes himself and his friends as "four who broke out of the human framework, left of their own accord toward freedom and found themselves united...['Simplism'] perhaps holds some analogy with that childhood state we seek—a state in which everything is simple, easy... The ease we're aiming toward is what theologians call grace." Daumal is perhaps still thinking of this "childhood state" in 1935, when he speculates that "the four-year-old child thinks absolutely; for him, fire eats, bread suffers when sliced, the furniture that knocks against him is mean..."

Despite his search for "grace" and its "poetic consequences," Daumal's life in Reims is largely that of the average "nonconformist" adolescent. His unfashionably long hair makes him an object of local ridicule; he plays tricks on neighbors, goes drinking, and dances in taverns. A constant air of self-mockery covers his shyness. "Papa" Lecomte, more at ease in such situations, frequently amazes his "son." Maurice Henry recalls that upon meeting Daumal and asking what his fellow townsmen thought of his behavior, the latter answered: "Here I'm considered the local clown."

But the Simplists' pranks also take more "experimental"—and dangerous—forms. Alone, Daumal walks for hours with eyes closed, somehow avoiding the obstacles in his path. He attempts to "see," while blindfolded, an object locked in a box or placed at some distance. With Lecomte, he tries to connect with "prenatal" memories, situations of déjà vu that they call "paramnesia." Lecomte, for his part, studies "vision by Epiphysis" (referring to the pineal gland which, in Theosophy, once served as our "third eye") and tries to demonstrate that "clairvoyance is man's natural state." These activities, among others, are so many aspects of what the group names "experimental metaphysics," defined by critic Michel Random as "a re-cognition of death (of what determines it)—and beyond that, the possibility of a non-death, or of the spirit's continuity."

If all of these "experiments" aim at a knowledge of the beyond in some form, the most direct are Daumal's brushes with suicide.

He declares in 1928: "to commit suicide surely proves (more or less?) that one holds to life; not to commit suicide *proves nothing.*" And the following year: "suicide is the most violent possible affirmation of the self." But Daumal's experience with suicide is not only theoretical; at age 17, "for lack of reasons to live," he tries to kill himself. "I suddenly feel my ties to my family," he later tells his doctor, "and my responsibility toward my younger brother." Earlier, during a Simplist game of Russian roulette, having drawn the short straw, he puts the gun to his head, pulls the trigger...and faints. In his essay "Nerval the Nyctalope," Daumal relates his vision at what he believed to be death's door:

> Do you remember the night in the park when you blew my brains out? I was sure of *leaving* and I had taken my departure from the world with an ease that astonished me. A recurring vision from my dreams surged from the chiming of the last bells... It showed immense marble stairs leading up a hill with its peak in splendor... Do you remember how I rolled on the ground when I realized that you had fooled me...?

And in the poem "Disillusion":

> White and black and white and black:
> careful now, I'm going to teach you how to die.
> Shut your eyes, grit your teeth,
> click! You see, it's not so hard,
> nothing to get worked up about...

But if suicide provides the most direct confrontation with death, it also holds the most obvious drawbacks. Another means of trying to reach the "beyond" is explored: drugs. The use of various narcotics and toxins constitutes perhaps the most prolonged aspect of the Simplists' "experimental metaphysics," and also highlights the fundamental contradiction between Daumal and Roger Gilbert-Lecomte. For Lecomte, drugs are a passage to a "pre-natal" state, a backward movement to a point between life and death, an escape from what he considers his "accidental birth" into the world. For Daumal, on the other hand, the question of death subsumes all else, is the only true subject of research, regardless of the means used.[2] "I do not hope for

2. Much later, Daumal will note that the revelation of drugs "determined [Lecomte's] life as it determined mine, albeit in a different direction."

v

Death," he writes to Maurice Henry in 1929, "I want to *possess it*... So long as my death is not my own doing, it will be but transitory." This period will see some of Daumal's most haunting and revelatory poetry about death, including the lines:

> ..."I am mortal." These words sweeten the void,
> for they mean: "I am yours."
> I am mortal! Mortal what I love in your name!
> But the day of my mortality is endless.

The will to "possess" death, to know it once and for all, leads Daumal to perform experiments with the carbon tetrachloride he used to collect beetles: "I decided to confront the problem of death itself: I would put my body in as close a state as possible to physiological death, but would concentrate my attention on staying awake and recording all that presented itself to me..." What Daumal sees in these trips to death's gate is a certainty that the "beyond" exists, that an "absurd evidence" lies past the limits of conscious life. His two essays "Asphyxiation and Absurd Evidence" (1930) and the more detailed "Determining Memory" (written in 1943 at Jean Paulhan's suggestion) relate this "fundamental experience" with astounding lucidity, and provide a key to the totality of Daumal's life-long research. Comparing the two is revelatory in this respect: "The Determining Memory," the product of a more mature mind informed by an entire corpus of esoteric knowledge, has nonetheless lost nothing of the earlier essay's awe before the phenomenon's sheer overpowering intensity.

The concept of "absurd evidence," furthermore, dominates the first half of Daumal's writings, taking on in them the value of a philosophical term (nonetheless keeping in mind, as Daumal does, that any verbal "term" is no more than a signpost of experience, and not the experience itself). "Evidence" means that which is *immediately* apparent, obvious, which strikes the mind as a sudden blinding light does the eye. Taking his cue from the ancient Hindu *ars poetica*, he will later define it as "that which pervades the heart as fire spreads through dry fuel." Its function is to "make something understood"– understood not in the intellectual sense of "grasping a concept," but in its very essence, an understanding which at once implicates both the intellectual and emotive faculties, and for which words can be but the crudest approximation. In his "Clavicles for a Great Poetic Game," written several years after the experience and

vi

placed at the head of *Le Contre-ciel* ("The Counter-Sky"), Daumal speaks of "the light" which "shines with the *Absurd Evidence*, with the painful certainty seeking the word so clearly undiscoverable, so simply ineffable, seeking the single Word which proclaims the Evidence absurd." And he warns: "He who *sees the absurd* suffers this torture: to have the Word-to-end-all-words on the tip of his tongue, but unutterable."

Paris: from Simplism to Grand Jeu.

In October 1925 Daumal goes to Paris to begin his studies at the prestigious Lycée Henri-IV, in preparation for entrance exams to the Ecole Normale Supérieure. He lives in quasi-exile from his friends, whose rare visits he awaits with impatience. Some consolation is afforded by his classes with noted philospher Emile Chartier, better known as "Alain." In a letter to his parents he writes: "Mr. Chartier...is very interesting, despite his strange manner and the loose way he conducts his courses." Chartier strongly influences the development of Daumal's writing and thought; the former pupil will later invoke these classes in "The Limits of Philosophical Language." During this time, Daumal begins in earnest his studies of Sanskrit, born out of a dissatisfaction with the existing translations of Hindu texts, and his poetic activity. He also suffers frequent hallucinations. "I was at least a hundred ft. from anyone...[I heard] women's voices right nearby: 'You're going to your death, darling...' —'He'll end up rubbing his nose in it...' and one amazing thing I should have written down, for I've forgotten it," he writes to Lecomte.

Scholastic vacations mean a return to his friends in Reims and their experiences of the beyond. It is at this point that Daumal, along with Meyrat, devotes himself to experiments in the "waking dream," attempts to project his "double" out of his sleeping physical shell and into the streets. In his essay on Nerval, he describes the process of separating his two "selves," and insists: "It was in a real world that I held nocturnal meetings with my friend, Robert Meyrat... Seen from outside, I was asleep. But in reality I was wandering effortlessly..." And yet one night, unexpectedly, Meyrat fails to appear, and his friends never see him again. Daumal in particular remains hurt and bewildered by what he considers Meyrat's betrayal. In a letter to Lecomte he writes: "Poor Robert. Why, why? Could we have strangled him? could he have strangled himself?" The tone with which he recounts the disappearance is all but elegaic.[3]

A further disappointment is caused by Lecomte who, although more and more frequently in Paris, seems to have little time for his friend, preferring the company of influential critic Léon Pierre-Quint and the Montparnasse literary (and narcotics) milieu. Flippancy reveals the hurt: "So it's understood: you take Spongefoot [Daumal] for a *minus habens;* or else you croaked in clandestine fashion... You leave me here in a trance; and I feel ashamed when someone asks how you are, and I have nothing to answer."

Daumal's academic projects take a turn in June 1927, on the morning of his exams, when a bad fall on the head leaves him without memory for several days. Plans for the Ecole Normale are abandoned in favor of "free" studies in philosophy at the Sorbonne. Daumal will come to view the accident as "fortuitous." He describes his life at this time: "I live with my parents, who have a place in the suburbs, but spend many nights out and lead a very irregular life. I continue to try all kinds of drugs (hashish) and begin to take opium. I stop in time, horrified by the sight of the addicts around me." In the fall, Daumal meets the painter Joseph Sima, who provides a visual dimension to the group's philosophical preoccupations, as well as Dutch writer Hendrick Cramer and his Siberian-born wife Vera Milanova (later Vera Daumal). Finally, in December, the poet André Rolland de Renéville joins the group.

Following the lead of various avant-garde movements (notably Surrealism), there is talk at this time of drafting a "Simplist manifesto." In 1926 Daumal writes to Meyrat and Lecomte of having composed "several snatches," including notes on Simplism's attitude toward religion, ethics, poetry, their differences with Surrealism, etc.[4] By early 1927 the manifesto has evolved into plans for a magazine, and the group begins preparing a first issue. A working title is chosen by Lecomte and

3. In 1961, Roger Vailland, ever the demystifier, will again see Meyrat, finding that "the Ghoul" has become a fastidious old doctor. "He visits Roger Gilbert-Lecomte's grave once a week... Remained in adolescence —ours—and never left Reims."

4. Although this manifesto will never be written, the fourth issue of *Le Grand Jeu* (unpublished) is devoted to an examination of the same problems.

Daumal: *La Voie* (the path, the way). However, it is Roger Vailland who gives the magazine – and the group – its definitive name. His journalistic flair leaves him unsatisfied with the quiet, spiritual "Path," preferring instead the flashier title *Le Grand Jeu:* the Big Game.

The Big Game.

By the time the first issue of *Le Grand Jeu* appears in 1928, the group is already able to present a clear notion of its guiding principles: the primacy granted to Poetry as closest possible expression of the Absolute; adherence to a political and aesthetic avant-garde, subtended by a return to ancient esoteric traditions; a marked iconoclasm *vis-à-vis* the dominant doctrines of Western civilization. A polemic statement by Daumal and Lecomte proclaims the group "shatterers of dogmas" ("DEFINITION:...'the *Grand Jeu* is entirely and systematically destructive'"), while Daumal's review of Lucien Lévy-Bruhl's work chides the anthropologist for attempting to grasp "primitive" thought with Western standards. In the second issue, he begins an essay on mystic thinker René Guénon with the words: "The essential pattern of my thought, of our thought, of thought is inscribed – as I have known for years – in the sacred books of India."

The tenets of Hindu philosophy take on increasing importance for Daumal, as he becomes more and more aware of the limitations imposed by Western approaches to knowledge. Some years later, he will define the difference by saying that, whereas the adult Westerner considers himself in full possession of his faculties which he can then apply to various objects, the Hindu considers the progress of knowledge "the acquisition and perfecting of new organs," and the *self* experimental, in transformation, "the fundamental object of all knowledge." Thus for Daumal, Western man's greatest weakness is his clinging to a fixed individuality, his belief that to "understand" an object is to isolate it. "The specific is revolting," he declares in 1929. It is this thinking, shaped by Hindu tradition, that leads him in the same year to write: "this individuality is my garment, it is not me... An individual is the *unlimited* thinking of itself as *limited*, thus deprived of itself."

Certain of Daumal's pronouncements, and the group's comportment in general, are not long in catching the eye of Surrealism, and overtures are made to individual members by

André Breton and friends. *Grand Jeu* partisans would have it that Breton was unwilling to let a group of youngsters so obviously "indebted" to Surrealism elude his control. But the *Grand Jeu*, while sympathetic to the basic principles of Surrealism ("We are Surrealists, nuances aside," Daumal tells Maurice Henry), finds much to criticize in its actual workings. Their reservations can be seen in part as 'adolescent revolt' against Breton's more established circle. But for the most part, the *Grand Jeu's* misgivings are based on some very real philosophical differences (including what they consider the decline of Surrealist discoveries into facile poetic "tricks"), and advances are politely but systematically refused. So it is that on March 11, 1929, Breton calls a meeting of the Parisian intellectual left at the Bar du Château, ostensibly to discuss Trotsky's recent banishment from the Communist Party. Proclaiming that no discussion can be initiated before determining the "moral qualifications" of those present, Breton begins a long inquest whose only object seems to be to discredit the *Grand Jeu*, criticizing each of its members, condemning in particular a newspaper article, signed by Vailland, in praise of a Paris police chief. (Although defended by his friends during the meeting, Vailland is soon after excluded from the *Grand Jeu* on the grounds that his journalism conflicts with the group's ideological tendencies.) Several months later, a magazine issue on Surrealism provides Breton with the chance to embellish his version of the proceedings, with ample space devoted to the *Grand Jeu's* "failings." And in the *Second Surrealist Manifesto*, all the while inviting Daumal to join the Surrealists, Breton deems it unfortunate "that Daumal has hitherto avoided stating in no uncertain terms his personal position and that of the *Grand Jeu*...with respect to Surrealism." With the publication of the "Open Letter," Breton gets his wish—and more than he bargained for. In it, Daumal clarifies his own dissatisfactions with Surrealism and his reasons for preferring the *status quo*, extends in turn an invitation to Breton (!), and concludes with the warning: "Beware of eventually figuring in study-guides to literary history." A warning that Breton would have done well to take more seriously; for if Surrealism is chiefly remembered today as an artistic and literary movement, the *Grand Jeu* has yet to be granted the condescending approval of encyclopedic classification.

Meetings with remarkable men.
Although the fourth issue of *Le Grand Jeu* is by now ready
for press, no. 3 will prove to be the last. Increasingly, Daumal
finds himself alone against various problems of magazine
finance and production, his own poverty and the battle against
drug addiction. He tells a friend: "I'm hesitating between despair
and philosophy." Gilbert-Lecomte's taste for morphine renders
him incapable of attending to the matters at hand, and Daumal
often finds himself acting as nurse to his friend (Vailland later
comments: "Daumal is playing the male protecting his mate").
His letters from this period reveal a desperate faith in their ability
to beat the monkey: 'I don't leave Roger's side, and it's a constant battle against the monster, enough to drive me crazy...But
But when Roger is ready, we'll really set things on fire." A profession of faith which is all the more pathetic in that Lecomte,
unable and unwilling to be cured, will eventually die of his
addiction.

It is likely that Daumal would have followed the same path
as his friend were it not for his meeting in late 1930 with Alexandre de Salzmann, of whom he writes: "he's restored my hope
and given me a reason to live... I'm beginning to reexamine my
values and put some order back into my life." With the *Grand
Jeu*'s activities tending more and more toward empty polemic
and frustration, Salzmann and his wife, disciples and colleagues
of G.I. Gurdjieff, appear to Daumal as the answer he has been
searching for. He quickly abandons the Paris literary scene and
acknowledges Salzmann as his "master" (that is, both "superior"
and "teacher"). To the skeptical Rolland de Renéville he states:
"a master is someone who gives you the chance to learn... A
'master' will never think *for* you: he will provide you with
chances to think, which you will or won't take advantage of..."

More than any other event, including André Breton's
manipulations, this encounter marks the final phase of the *Grand
Jeu*, the other members proving unable to accept Daumal's sudden conversion. (Vailland disdainfully remarks on "the superior
smile of the believer" after his last meeting with Daumal.) He
explains to Jean Paulhan:

> Our situation is that of shipwrecked men about to drown.
> By their own efforts, they've managed so far to keep their
> heads above water. By his own efforts, man can go up to
> a certain point. If no outside help comes, he'll drown...

Someone's thrown me a life preserver. Should I start quibbling?

By 1932 it is clear that the *Grand Jeu* is dissolving, and that Lecomte is incapable of carrying on. Vera, with whom Daumal has fallen in love, is in the United States.[5] When he meets Indian dancer Uday Shankar and is offered a job as his press secretary, Daumal leaves with the troupe for New York. While there he joins Vera and begins writing *La Grande beuverie* ("A Night of Serious Drinking"), a fictional send-up of Parisian intelligentsia that can be seen as the closing chapter of his own life to this point. Various essays over the next several years— particularly "On the Life of Basiles"—provide a wry commentary on the sham and pretense Daumal now sees even in the *Grand Jeu*'s most sincere quest for "truth."

Limits of philosophical language.

When Daumal returns to France in early 1933, little is left of the *Grand Jeu*. He nonetheless maintains contact with most of his friends and brings Lecomte, now totally dependent on morphine and Daumal's care, to live in the small apartment he and Vera have rented. His financial condition is desperate—his only source of income being translations (including Hemingway's *Death in the Afternoon*) and contributions to reviews—and he is exempted from military service on grounds of poor health. Lecomte, for his part, pursues a constant cycle of hospitals, detoxification and return to his Montparnasse pushers. Finally despairing of any cure for him, Daumal breaks definitively with the friend who has been so strong an influence on his life. Some years later he writes to Jean Paulhan: "I learned that no one could make *my* effort for me, and that I could not make someone else's effort for him; I learned to hate lies." And when in 1941 he speaks of the "black poet" whose poetic seed "remains dark and produces blind, subterranean vegetation," it is certainly with Lecomte in mind.

In essence, Daumal, whose life contains a series of devotions to various guides, is abandoning one master for another. For by this time he and Vera have become dedicated pupils of Gurd-

5. There is little available documentation tracing their relationship, but by 1928 Daumal's letters already attest to a deep affection for Vera. By the time Cramer abandons her in 1931, she and Daumal are already engaged in what seems to have been a marriage of true minds.

jieff's teaching, as transmitted by Alexandre and Jeanne de Salzmann. We could argue that Daumal had in fact been seeking such a master for many years. Already in his 1926 story "Old Mugle," he wrote of a fictional meeting with a figure strongly resembling both Salzmann and (for his hold over Daumal) Roger Gilbert-Lecomte; and in a poem from *Le Contre-ciel* he speaks of "a pitiless teacher with a smile like glowing ice [who] offers me another body." When Salzmann dies in May, René and Vera join his widow in Switzerland to pursue their "education." An essay on "The Role of Movement in the Complete Education of Man," written in 1934 as propaganda for Mme. de Salzmann's classes, describes the reasons for his attachment.

What Daumal sees in the Teaching is an opportunity to reconnect the truncated fragments of his being, to address his "head, heart and belly" as one. Almost ten years before he stated that "the great teachers of men addressed neither their senses, their hearts nor their intelligence in particular; they spoke to each man's entire being." Mme. de Salzmann's tutelage, in other words, is less a break with, than an extension of, his experiences with the *Grand Jeu*.

The second vital aspect of the Teaching is that "knowledge" is never presented as such; that is, the students are never *told* to accept something as true. Rather, knowledge is offered indirectly, often through a series of gestures (movement), and it is the task of each one to receive and understand it on his own terms. Daumal later writes to Georges Ribemont-Dessaignes: "I told you that I've encountered in my life a veritable teaching. One sign of its truth, for me, is that it never offers a pre-established path." In general, the Teaching forces Daumal to "prepare the edifice" to receive wisdom—preparation which will become a recurrent image in his work and his major preoccupation in the face of mortality. In his prize-winning collection of poems, *Le Contre-ciel* (the jury for which includes Gide, Valéry and Giraudoux), he writes: "Learning *not* to daydream, but to think; learning *not* to philosophize, but to speak—this is not accomplished in one day. And yet we have but few days in which to do it."

How to *say* something is a problem Daumal seeks to resolve, paradoxically, by exploring the non-verbal ways in which knowledge is imparted. His long-time distrust of words as carriers of thought, sanctioned by Hindu tradition and the Teaching, spawns a series of essays which attempt to define just how far one can go with verbal language. One of these, Daumal's masterwork on "The Limits of Philosophical Language," speaks notably of the constant doubt imposed by Socratic dialectics, and of the life-long training undergone by the Vedic brahman—training which, through a series of commentaries on a single text, eventually leads the brahman back to his point of origin! What is fundamental in this teaching, Daumal realizes, is not the object of knowledge (which remains the same), but the brahman's evolving understanding of it: although his words at the end of his life are identical to those at the beginning, the internal force behind them is infinitely greater. In a letter to Renéville, Daumal admits: "in the domain of words, the ancient Hindus beat around the bush like everyone else," but were nonetheless "a bit closer to it." For Daumal, thought is not word but *act*; and the highest act is found at that silent point where Being begins—what Eliot calls "the still point of the turning world." "One does not know speech by means of words," Daumal writes in 1936, "but through silence."

Sèvres and mountains.

The years 1936 and 1937 see Daumal living between Mme. de Salzmann's home in the Paris suburb of Sèvres—where he and Vera have a room—and the Alps. An ardent mountain climber, Daumal experiences the peaks both as a physical obstacle to be conquered by force of will and as a spiritual revelation. He tells Vera: "On the peaks, thought is substantial or is not at all... I understand why the Chinese sages, Christ, Moses, the followers of Shiva and others went up to the summits to think." *Mount Analogue,* an allegorical account of the Teaching told in Alpinistic terms, shows to what extent Daumal considers his two activities of this time to be part of the same fundamental quest. Again to Vera, he expresses the relation: "in difficult passes, you talk to the mountain, you insult it...you beg it, you flatter it, you promise it all kinds of things—and in fact, I must say that it finally works: it's a way of speaking to your own nature by pretending to speak to external nature. It's the great natural comedy."

In Sèvres, Daumal pursues his education with equal ardor, despite the fatigue occasioned by intense mental and gymnastic activity—fatigue aggravated by the worsening condition of his lungs, which his earlier use of CCl_4 has seriously damaged.

The "courses" consist of various exercises, including games of *"freeze!,"* whirling dervish dances (to music composed by Gurdjieff), close scrutiny of familiar gestures, backward counting and attentive prayer.[6] Although the details of these sessions are kept secret—in "The Role of Movement" Daumal speaks only in vague terms—numerous veiled references to the activities can be found in his texts from this time on, including a poke at his more mundane household chore of maintaining the furnace.

In 1938, through Jeanne de Salzmann, Daumal first meets Gurdjieff in the Café de la Paix. He is not spared the Russian's typical barrage of humorous insults and booming guffaws. Far from taking offense, however, he recognizes in these mannerisms the pataphysical laughter he had celebrated nearly ten years before. Jean Biès speaks of the affinity between "the long-haired young man dragging his will to Knowledge down the bourgeois streets... and the ersatz carpet dealer, holding court in cafés and loading his amazing stories with arabesques of mockery." Daumal is too old a hand at showmanship not to recognize Gurdjieff's comedy, which provides an amusing contrast to the high seriousness of the Teaching. He considers his few meetings with "the master" less a revelation than the confirmation of what he has known all along; and it is startling to see the tone of these encounters so accurately anticipated in an early poem:

> Death with its vulgar laugh
> behind green shutters
> sucks on an English candy,
> and the carpets are wet with mint tea.

It is also at Mme. de Salzmann's insistence that Daumal, whose health has been deteriorating visibly, consents to see a doctor. Examination reveals advanced tuberculosis in both lungs. Daumal returns to the Alpine air, but refuses any formal treatment. To Ribemont-Dessaignes he quips: "I often suffered from not knowing, when I didn't want to accomplish some action, whether it was cowardly laziness or legitimate fatigue... Now I simply need a thermometer: up to 99.5 it's laziness; above, it's illness." It is on these peaks that he begins his unfinished masterpiece, *Mount Analogue,* "a novel of symbolically authentic non-Euclidean adventures" dedicated to the memory of Alex-

---

6. Cf. the poem "The Invisible Man" in "Some French Poets of the XXVth Century," which closely follows the spirit of these sessions.

andre de Salzmann. "With this mountain for my language," he says, "I will speak of another mountain which is the life uniting the earth and sky, and I will speak of it not to resign myself, but to urge myself onward."

Poetry black, poetry white.

The outbreak of war in 1939 marks the end of the Sèvres group. The following year, Daumal joins Mme. de Salzmann in the unoccupied zone hoping to revive the "classes," but she is anxious to return to Gurdjieff in Paris, and Daumal and Vera are soon left alone. At this point they live in extreme poverty, Daumal's minimal income deriving from free-lance editorial work and the 1938 publication of *La Grande beuverie*. A further problem is posed by Vera's Jewish origins and naturalized American status. Plans are made for an escape to New York, but the couple decides instead on marriage, thus giving her French citizenship.

During this period, Daumal suddenly returns to poetic composition after a ten-year lapse, and writes his fundamental study, "Poetry Black, Poetry White." In a scant five pages, this essay offers the fruit of twenty years' intensive research and experience, constituting one of the most moving and useful descriptions of the poetic art to be written in this century. True to the principles he has supported in one form or another all of his life, Daumal refuses to give a "recipe" for poetry—for this would be merely to create another of the "thinking machines" denounced by the *Grand Jeu*. And yet, it is impossible for anyone who considers himself a poet to read this essay without feeling somehow enriched, or without recognizing more clearly the various tendencies of his own work. In the same fashion, Daumal does not point to examples of "black" or "white" poets, but simply concludes: "if I was once a poet, I was certainly a black poet; and if tomorrow I must be a poet, I wish to be a white one."

By 1943 Daumal has changed residence six times in two years. An alarmed Gurdjieff warns him: "At this point, your task is to heal." Nonetheless, in the fall, unable to remain separated from his master, Daumal braves the dangers of the Occupation and the difficulties of travel to return to Paris. Recounting this episode, Georges Ribemont-Dessaignes notes that Daumal "threw his dice in the air: either mind or body! The body sank..."

And yet it is precisely because the two cannot be split that Daumal feels he must make his journey. "Remember the two sides of the coin," he writes in 1942, "—and its single metal." Frequent relocation, undernourishment and lack of treatment take their toll: his condition worsens steadily, leaving him thin and bedridden. But the boy whose fear of death "clawed at his stomach," at age 36 faces the certainty of his impending mortality with the calm of a monk setting himself ablaze.

News reaches Daumal of Gilbert-Lecomte's death on the last day of 1943. He writes to a friend: "I am convinced that he has now been given another chance."

The early months of 1944 are devoted entirely to the writing of *Mount Analogue*. According to Vera Daumal, a visitor knocking on the door causes Daumal to interrupt his novel in midsentence. It will progress no further, for on May 21 he succumbs in his bed, leaving in his notes the final question, typically unanswered: "And you—what do you seek?"

In 1956, Roger Vailland enters in his diary a grudging yet fitting epitaph for his two former comrades: "René Daumal and Roger Gilbert-Lecomte died from having pursued our alchemy of happiness too rigorously... I honor their fidelity to our youth."

Many have sought "the truth" and have tried to impart this truth through their writings. It is Daumal's peculiar lucidity which made him realize early on that verbal language could go only so far, that there existed a corpus of traditional knowledge which had struggled with this problem, and that this knowledge could be reinterpreted—indeed, its very nature requires constant interpretation—to fit the particular trials of the modern age, our own specific "truths." Among Daumal's notebooks, we find the following admonition: "Even without wanting to, you always leave a few traces. Be ready to answer to your fellow men for the trail you leave behind you." Daumal's essays provide not only a document of exceptional literary craft and impact, but precisely one of the most "answerable" trails of his time, a carefully rendered map of the path he painstakingly forged.

*   *   *   *   *   *

These essays are presented, as well as could be ascertained, in an order following the chronology of their composition—

thus, of the development of Daumal's thought. The text follows that of Gallimard's two-volume *Essais et notes* (with original publication consulted where possible), except for "Draft of an Introduction..." which first appeared in *Cahiers de l'Herne* no. 10 (1968). Footnotes indicated by a number are Daumal's; those indicated by an asterisk, mine.

For the data used in this introduction, I have referred primarily to Jean Biès' monograph, *René Daumal* (Paris, 1967), and Michel Random's two-volume essay on *Le Grand Jeu* (Paris, 1970; the most complete study of the group to date), as well as to private correspondence and various articles "in memory of."

Finally, for their help in the preparation of these manuscripts, I would like to thank Bill Zavatsky, Jodi Daynard, Claudio Rugafiori and the late Maurice Henry.

M.P.
Paris-New York, 1985.

THE ABSURD EVIDENCE

FREEDOM WITHOUT HOPE

The sunken, shining eye sees doors everywhere, and man rushes headlong toward them, face forward. He sees empty sky and open spaces. For him every object is a sign of power. But which will he choose? Tyrannical gods come to guide and tempt him: desire, interest, love, beauty, reason. He wants to choose freely and for himself. He will no longer accept a motive for acting. For him every goal is a master. He wants to want for the sake of wanting, to act according to pure dictates. The "gratuitous act," he says, is the only free act; and the only value the human soul can house is the will that, neither guided by reason nor directed toward an end, freely decides on action.

This is where the spirit of revolt begins to die. For as soon as a man thinks he has discovered within himself a road to explore or a new reality to attain, actions become indifferent and the world foreign. He who has reached this point moves in the world and accomplishes the acts natural to man with the constant thought: "Since I am so different from all these creatures who are supposedly my equals, since I am an angel and this is the only thing that matters, what's the use of acting differently from anyone else?" At the same time, he sees that to act against a given law is still to obey that law, that to act systematically against desire is still to give in to desire; the pull of gravity is what causes the balloon to rise away from Earth. This man—who feels that he is such only by disguise—tells himself with an inner laugh, at each of his actions: "I am really acting like a man."

He does not laugh at these actions with the abject laugh of the defeated, but with the desperate laugh of the man who, on the verge of committing suicide, judges it futile to pull the trigger. This divorce from the world, which makes the mind feel indifferent toward it, is often close to despair—but a despair that laughs at the world. If the mind removes itself from things, at the same time the body removes itself from other bodies;

1

its stiffening isolates it, and covers the face with the muscular mask of irony. A man in revolt believes he has found peace and often even believes he can keep it for life. But there he is: caught behind his rigid mask of scorn. The mind takes on the habit of saying to everything the body does or experiences, "It's not important." And man believes he has found salvation. Existence and worldly goods lose their value, nothing is to be feared, and the soul continues its search for purity in this stiffening of stoic pride.

Only one thing matters, says the man who has reached this point, and that is inner peace. He believes he can achieve it through that resistance of the will which refuses to be part of human life. But nothing can enrich the soul in this exile, for it has only folded over onto itself; in its abstract prison, it is as cut off from Heaven as it is from Earth. Heavy boredom and dryness, with their parade of temptations, make it feel its immobility and drowsiness.

One evening, man leans out of his window and looks at the countryside. Things pale and swarming, haze or spectres, come out of the ploughed earth and slip toward the houses; a cat imitates the death-rattle of a strangled child, and the dogs in the moonlight rediscover the great voice of the steppenwolf in the back of their throats. Man at his window feels a monstrous, savage, animal desire welling up—the desire to go out and howl and dance in the moonlight, to run shivering under this foreign light, to venture all the way up to the houses and spy on the slumber of men, and perhaps make away with a sleeping child. An animal, a wolf is reborn in him and grows, swells his throat and his breast. He is going to howl. —No! He is strong! With a sudden movement he jerks backward, closes the window, and tries to convince himself that he was only dreaming. But something knots up in the pit of his stomach, as before, in his childhood, when he thought about death. He is afraid. But this is not worthy of him. Isn't he armed against it? "What does it matter?" he tries to tell himself. Still, he doubts. He goes to bed; but if he tries to resist this anguish, he will not be able to sleep. Little by little he loses his self-confidence. He gives in to somnolence, and immediately the demons make their entry: as bedfellows he will have the leprous, noseless succubus, the frog-man who stinks of fish and the ignoble head, swollen with purple blood, that balances on its webbed feet. The scorned world takes its revenge on his constricted throat, his hesitantly beating heart, his stomach into which the monsters sink their claws. In the morning, he finds his faith in himself badly shaken. Temptations of suffering, fear or boredom summon the soul to overcome them or to let itself be crushed. He who receives them is lucky, for he may recognize his error. An abstract solution solves nothing: man is saved in his entirety or not at all. Only understanding can split him into body and mind; for understanding knows and methodically separates to provide an object for itself. Nor is an abstract solution any good for a society; the same mechanism of repression applies. One sees nations, apparently well-policed, in which there is merely a repression of instincts that barely manage to surface under the violent constraints of strict law-enforcement. On the other hand, these instincts are given free reign in those who can most easily avoid punishment, such as the police themselves. These men become the instruments of an awakening animal cruelty. In police stations, these defenders of law and order tie up a man who has been arrested under some pretext in a public demonstration, tear out his eyes, rip off his ears with their fists, or scorch the soles of his feet until he confesses to whatever it is they want. Such signs indicate that this society has not been able to master the poisons developing in its breast, most likely because it seeks to resolve the problem of justice by applying inappropriate solutions to the question of human relations. It is a warning that this society is at the mercy of the slightest breakdown; and society is lucky if it can recognize these signs! So it is for the individual: after these revelations, he must find the faith he thought he already had.

The basis of this haughty scorn of the world is immense pride. Man wanted to affirm his existence apart from humanity, and in so doing he became subject not only to the pride that froze his spirit in the single-minded affirmation of the self, but also to the power of the world he wanted to scorn. His only deliverence is to give himself totally to each action, instead of pretending to accept being a man. Let the body slip among other bodies along the path that has been traced for it, let man flow among other men following the laws of nature. The body must be given to Nature, passions and desires to the animal, thoughts and sentiments to man. By this giving, everything that forms the individual is returned to the unity of existence. And the soul, which constantly surpasses all form and is only a soul at this price, is returned to the unity of divine essence by the same simple act of self-denial. This unity, recovered in two aspects and in a single act that joins them, I call *God*, God in three persons.

The essence of renunciation is to accept everything while denying everything. Nothing that has a form is me; but the determining factors of my individuality are thrown back on the world. *Freedom is not free will, but a liberation;* it is the negation of individual autonomy. The soul refuses to model itself on the image of the body, of desires, of reason; actions become natural phenomena; and man acts the way lightning strikes. In whatever form I find myself, I must say: *that is not me.* By this negation, I throw all form back to created Nature, and make it appear as object. I want to leave whatever tends to limit me—body, temperament, desires, beliefs, memories—to the sprawling world, and at the same time to the past, for this act of negation creates both consciousness and the present; it is a single and eternal act of the instant. Consciousness is perpetual suicide. If it knows itself in duration, it is nonetheless only *present*—that is, a simple, immediate act, beyond duration.

Space is the form common to all these objects; an object is what is not me; *space is the universal tomb, not the image of my freedom.* When the horizon ceases to be the receding image of freedom, when it is no more than a bar placed before the eyes and man feels himself guided by the hands of space, then he will begin to know what it means to be free. There is no room between bodies for freedom. It is only when he stops searching for freedom that man frees himself. True resignation is that which, in the same act, gives itself to God, body and soul.

But to talk of resignation is not a charm which suddenly leads to the discovery of peace and happiness. Very often, those who believe they have mastered inner calm are not the resigned, but the weak. They repeat the few rules they have been taught like stupefying charms, and thus live in abject tranquility. They accept everything but deny nothing, and by consent want to live only a life adorned with elusive hopes that humor their cowardice. Resignation can only be the voluntary abandonment of a possible revolt. The man resigned must be ready to revolt at all times; otherwise, peace will settle into his life and he will sleep, starting once more to consent to everything. The act of renunciation is not accomplished once and for all, but is a perpetual sacrifice of revolt.

This is why it is dangerous to preach humility to weak souls: it only removes them further from themselves. The individual, frozen and folded into himself, can only become aware of his destiny in revolt. It is the same for society. As the individual closes himself up to sleep like a coward behind the ramparts of hopes and pledges, so society limits itself in the walls of institutions. The individualist seeks peace by closing himself into solid, clear-cut boundaries—as does the nationalist state. Both of them can only find their true path, the path on which they can freely advance, in the revolt that goes beyond limits. Man and society must constantly be on the point of exploding, must constantly renounce this explosion, must always refuse to stop at a defined form. Freedom means giving oneself over to the necessity of Nature, and true will is only that of a fulfilled action. *This resignation, as opposed to abjection, is power itself,* for the body returned to the world then participates in the whole of Nature. The Russian *Nichevo* lets us understand the success of Marxism in Russia.— *"It's nothing"*; that is, none of what pushes me to act is me. And the effort of will is not the desire to carry out an action, but to let it happen in continual detachment. To accept historical materialism was, for the Russian revolutionaries, to find freedom.

Before reaching renunciation, man always passes through these three stages: first, stupid acceptance of every rule, every convention, which grants him rest; then revolt in all its forms: struggle against society, misanthropy, escape into the desert, Pyrrhonism; and finally resignation, which never stops recognizing the power of revolt as constant.

Renunciation is an incessant destruction of all the shells that the individual seeks to put on. When man, tired of this labor, which is harder than revolt, is lulled to sleep in a facile peace, this shell thickens, and only violence can crack it open. To constantly reject all the crutches of hope, break all the stable creations of pledges, ceaselessly torment all desires, and never be sure of victory; such is the hard and sure path of renunciation.

We must make men despair, so that they may throw their humanity into the vast tomb of Nature, and so that, by abandoning their human nature to its own laws, they may leave it behind.

(1927-28.)

DRAFT OF AN INTRODUCTION TO THE *GRAND JEU*

The *Grand Jeu* gathers men whose only search is an absolute, immediate, implacable *evidence*, which has killed off any other concerns they might have had once and for all.

The *Grand Jeu* gathers men who have but one *Word* to say, tirelessly, in a thousand different tongues and always the same: the same *Word* as uttered by the Vedic Rishis, the Cabbalist Rabbis, the prophets, the mystics, the great heretics of all time and the true Poets.

The *Grand Jeu* seeks to lead a struggle with no reprieve and no mercy, on all levels, against those who betray this revelation for selfish human, individual or social interests:

priests,
scientists,
artists.

The *Grand Jeu* demands a *Revolution of Reality returning to its source*, a revolution which is fatal to all organizations defending degraded and contradictory forms of Being. It is thus the natural enemy of Countries, Imperialist States, Ruling Classes, Religions, Universities, and Academies.

For the *Grand Jeu*, the only true knowledge is the immediate identification of subject to object, the only true freedom liberation through a recognition of determined universal necessity.

No more free will!

No more whim or fantasy!

No more pretty things!

The *Grand Jeu* is *primitive, savage, ancient, realistic.*

(unpublished tract, ca. 1927)

6

INTRODUCTION TO THE *GRAND JEU*

The *Grand Jeu* is not a literary, artistic, philosophical or political review. The *Grand Jeu* seeks only the essential. The essential is like nothing we could imagine. The contemporary Western world has forgotten this oh-so-simple truth, and to find it again we must brave several dangers, the best known and most common of which are death (true death, that of the stone or of hydrogen, and not the pleasant kind, gorged with hope and decorated with exciting remorse, the kind of death we all know too well), madness (true madness, luminous and impotent like the sun lighting an assembly of magistrates, madness without issue, of he who is beaten down like a dog, and not the happy madness which is the most charming way of spending one's life), syphillis, leprosy, marriage or religious conversion.

Not only are those who play the *Grand Jeu* constantly on the verge of succumbing to the fear of playing with loaded dice, but they continuously risk the torments of the man who, wishing to cut off his hands with a hatchet, first cuts off his left hand and then doesn't know how to cut off the right, the more hated of the two. (Some call this situation a *compromise.*)

In this march toward a common land whose name will perhaps be revealed one day, the members of the *Grand Jeu* make — as if by coincidence — a certain number of discoveries which could interest, amuse, terrify or mortify the public. We impart them all.

Above all, we want to make men despair of themselves and of society. From this massacre of hopes, a bloody and pitiless Expectation will be born: eternal Being through refusal of the desire to last. Our discoveries are those of the explosion and dissolution of everything organized. For all organization perishes when goals are erased from the horizon of the future, which is no more than a white bar placed on one's forehead.

In this way, the idols men adore — knowing not why nor how — will crumble. It is useless to name them: they poison the air.

The ghouls that the *Grand Jeu* nourishes in warehouses reserved for this use know how to feed on these cadavers—for they do not make gods of their stomachs.

N.B.—For those who ask us about the *Grand Jeu*, we answer once and for all to any and every question: "Yes and no." We are thus the first to make the vanity of speech good for something. Moreover, we would not withhold advice from those who have the courage to question us without foolishness or mental restriction.

(1927-28.)

THE "SOUL" OF THE PRIMITIVE[1]

Here are pieces of thought ripped still living from the heart of the jungle and flung among us like masses of snakes. I read this with the same distress as when I hear a dream recounted. One man is a shark; a witch changes into a she-wolf; and I have always known that by loving a form, I become that form: human, animal or rock-face. I participate in what I love. Could Mr. Lévy-Bruhl be so incapable of love as to be ignorant of talismans, rings or handkerchiefs, the bewitchments and charms used by even the narrowest of loves: that of one human being for another?

But the logician's profession has made his hands too insensitive to caress these blood-filled mythologies, beautiful as cathedrals, without breaking them. He seriously states that the speculative curiosity of the Australians is "easily satisfied by myths." But mythological thought is the only primary living thought in man.[2] Logic is a technique; words are its tools. Thus

---

1. By Lucien Lévy-Bruhl [English trans. by L.A. Claire; London: Macmillan, 1928].

2. *Demonstration:*

1) Thought is grasped in an infinite number of forms. But thought in action is one, indivisible and eternal; only form is able to take on opposite qualities.

2) What I call my specific thoughts are only the specific forms in which thought is grasped.

3) Therefore, all human thought exists only in the contemplation of a specific form; and I have the idea of a form only insofar as I think this form.

4) Man seeks above all to know his destiny; still unable to *be* what he is tending to *become,* he can only outline and mimic.

5) This mimicry first takes the form of dance, before fatigue makes it a more intimate — and especially more vocal — movement; this internal dance, thought, is thus the imagining of a future form.

6) This is mythology, man's first and only spontaneous thought: thought which simultaneously affirms Form and Mind.

the logician (and Mr. Lévy-Bruhl is one when he judges primitive beliefs) believes he has control over all discourses, and then over all thought. Mr. Lévy-Bruhl thinks logically, he does not possess the thought of logic: lack of criticism. He confuses reality with things legitimately affirmed; the reality of mythological thought is not in the objects that its discourses affirm, but is rather that thought itself. The same error makes him oppose the savages' beliefs to an imaginary Catholicism which absolutely separates Mind from Matter. He does not understand that we are no more surprised by tales of lycanthropy and witchcraft than by the dogmas of Resurrection or Transubstantiation.

Furthermore, the author's lame commentary only appears from time to time, with its ridiculous insistence on translating the words *soul, spirit, shade, ghost* as "the dead man" or "the corpse." He makes me laugh as would a child in a museum who, seeing no more of the statues than their feet, timidly sketches repetitive little cartoon figures on them.

We know that the Mind is one, that the thought of a Bantu or an Eskimo is just as much our own. I find that image of a dead man coming downstairs on his head living in my skin; I could have dreamt it. There is a universality of myth. Primitive beliefs concerning metempsychosis can be found in Egyptian and Hindu theology; manifested in them is the love that shatters boundaries.

In answer to the methodical dualism of discursive science, an old Bergdamara says, "You separate them too much in your thoughts. For us, it all goes together." Lévy-Bruhl immediately sees a chasm between that mind and his own. Thus could a carpenter take me for a savage because I am unfamiliar with the basic rules of his trade. In the same way, Mr. Lévy-Bruhl's thought is a piece of wood, with a technique for hammering nails.

(Simply from the sociological viewpoint, how could he not understand the clan's universal tendency to wish that its dead members could be reincarnated back into its breast? The child, before being named, is superhuman: whence the respect he is shown. The name imposes fixed social responses upon him, and he is humanized. The balance of reactions between individuals is preserved by names, which epitomize the various affections caused in one being by another. The mind is one; form is desired as constant; which is the same as saying that a mind returns to live again in that form.)

(1928.)

MORE ON THE BOOKS OF RENE GUENON[1]

The essential pattern of my thought, of our thought, of thought is inscribed — as I have known for years — in the sacred books of India. Without fail, I come across each of my discoveries, shortly after having made it, in a verse of an *Upanishad* or of the *Bhagavad Gita* that I had not yet noticed. This necessarily induces me to trust in these Words, in the single Word that spawned them and in the mystic tradition that flows from them.

All moments of real and total thought are there: the lightning flash of metaphysics; the trample of dialectics' enormous clogs, which kill and revive; the necessary order imposed by criticism on the cadavers of thought; finally, a morality in which concessions to strictly human interest are so rare and so voluntarily exoteric that they fool no one.

But Western hands change gold into lead. Hindu metaphysics crumbles between these fat red fingers, becoming curiosities from mythology and exoticism, consoling searches for a specific paradise, little salutary words of advice that even a clergyman would not object to, love-cries toward certain entities, such as Nothingness, whose dark faces conceal the most fearsome hopes. We cannot really understand the first thing about Hindu thought if we have not grasped the whole in the original purity of a single spiritual act. The multiple edifice only makes sense in the unity and simplicity of the fire glowing from its rooftops.

Now, René Guénon never betrays Hindu thought for the particular needs of Western philosophy (philosophy of science, foundation of morals, politics, aesthetics, etc.). If he speaks of the Veda, he thinks the Veda, he *is* the Veda. Perhaps there are

---

1. I am specifically thinking of *L'Homme et son devenir selon le Vedanta* [Man and his becoming according to the Vedanta] (Paris, 1925), which I have just read.

11

errors or mistaken interpretations in his books; I don't know. But certainly he does not betray. To my knowledge, he is the only one not to, among those who have written on Hindu metaphysics. He has become so exclusively imbued with the original spirit of the Traditions we claim along with him that, because of this assimilation, what is deepest in European thinkers such as Spinoza, Hegel or the German post-Kantians completely escapes him.

It matters little. I prefer to see him keeping to that strict law, which is palpable in the tone of his sentences and keeps him from all compromise. He is thus sure of sacrificing nothing to those modern idols: discursive science, morals, progress, happiness of humanity, individual autonomy, life, life seen through rose-colored glasses, all this iron and absurd granite that weighs on our chests.

For these idols exist and they are heavy, and the transformation we seek should be able to break them; break them first, and in order to do this our human appearance shows the face of revolt. René Guénon, I know nothing of your strictly human life; I only know that you have little hope of convincing the masses. But I fear that the joy of thinking sometimes distracts you from this law—historical in the widest sense—which necessarily impels the man in me toward revolt: a revolt we consider not as an assigned task, but as work to be done by the human envelopes we absurdly call "ours." We want to free ourselves by letting the contingent forms of our beings seek their own destinies. We can say along with you that "these manifestations are directly related to the specific conditions of the Kali-Yuga." But as a man, aren't you yourself also subject to these conditions?

"It is impossible that scandals should not come..." But we refuse to add the revolting word of Christ, "...but woe unto him through whom they come!" Quite the contrary: by letting them come, we are delivered. Since those men who carry our names are agents of revolt, rather let us speak to them as Krishna to the warrior: "happy are the *kshatriyas* to whom opportunities for battle come unsought, opening for them the doors of the heavenly planets"[2]; and, for the most real in myself: "it is not I who act."[3]

(1928.)

2. *Bhagavad Gita*, II, 32.
3. *Ibid.*, V, 8.

To the reader unfamiliar with Alfred Jarry and the science called "pataphysics," the following essay could seem disorienting, not to say infuriatingly arcane. This is partly its intention. However, since the French reader of Daumal would most likely have at least a passing knowledge of Jarry's work, it is only fair that his English-speaking counterpart be given the same chance.

Cycling fanatic, absinthe-drinker of distinction and one of the most inventive minds in modern theater, Alfred Jarry (1873-1907) is best known as the author of the celebrated *Ubu* plays. Pataphysics, for its part, is less a literary creation than the overriding spirit of Jarry's life and work. We could call it the Science to correct science, or, as Jarry says, "the science of imaginary solutions." In *Exploits and Opinions of Doctor Faustroll, Pataphysician* (1911), he defines it as "the science of the particular, despite the common opinion that the only science is that of the general." Pataphysics – or 'pataphysics, "preceded by an apostrophe so as to avoid an easy pun'– is to physics and metaphysics what the monkey's face is to brass door-knockers: at once an absurd addition and an essential feature. Its influence is evident in such modern currents as Surrealism (André Breton considered Jarry one of the movement's founding fathers) and Absurdist drama, from Beckett and Ionesco to Monty Python's Flying Circus. But as Daumal and others have been quick to point out, even Socrates had his moments of pataphysical reasoning.

Roger Shattuck has described our science as "a method, a discipline, a faith, a cult, a point of view, a hoax. It is all of these and none of them." But perhaps just as clear an idea of what *it* is can be had from Jarry's own titles: "On the Futility of the 'Theatrical' in the Theater," "Faustroll Smaller than Faustroll," "The Passion Considered as an Uphill Bicycle Race." And so on.

Readers interested in exploring the subject further can consult the issue of *The Evergreen Review* (May-June 1960) entitled "What is 'Pataphysics?" and the chapter on Alfred Jarry in Shattuck's *The Banquet Years*. Jarry's works in English include *Ubu Roi* (New York: New Directions, 1961), *The Ubu Plays* (New York: Grove Press, 1969) and *The Supermale* (New York: New Directions, 1977). *Faustroll* appears in its entirety in *The Selected Works of Alfred Jarry,* edited by Roger Shattuck and Simon Watson Taylor (New York: Grove Press, 1965). I have slightly modified their translations for this essay.

PATAPHYSICS AND THE REVELATION OF LAUGHTER

"Pataphysics is the science..."
—Alfred Jarry, *Exploits and Opinions of
Dr. Faustroll, Pataphysician,* XLI.

For I know and I maintain that pataphysics is not simply a
joke. And if laughter often shakes the bones of us other
pataphysicians, it is a terrible laughter, faced with the evidence
that each thing is (and so arbitrarily!) just what it is and not
otherwise; that I *am* without being *everything,* that this is grotesque, and that all defined existence is scandalous.

In bodily terms, the shake of laughter is the jostling of bone
and muscle disintegrated by the great wave of anxiety and love-
panic as it penetrates the intimate interior of every last atom.
And then! under this slap in the face delivered by the absolute,
fragments of the pataphysician leap into the skin of the average
guy and rush headlong toward the maddening lies of the infinite roads of space, finally toward chaos. The individual who
has known himself in his totality can momentarily believe that
he is about to scatter into dust—a dust so homogenous that it
will be no more than dust, precisely filling an absence of dust,
in no place, and at no time. This happy earthling explodes, but
his all-too-solid elastic bag of skin holds him in, creases only
in the supplest parts of his face, pulls back the corners of his
mouth, tightens up at the eyelids and, distended to the extreme,
suddenly contracts and doubles up with a start, while his lungs
alternately fill with air and empty out. Thus is born the rhythm
of laughter, thought and felt in itself, or as it is observed in the
laughing other. Each time he thinks he will explode once and
for all, man is held back by his *skin,* I mean by his *form;* by the
bonds of his specific law whose form is external expression;
by the absurd formula, the irrational, unresolved equation of
his existence. He constantly rebounds off that absolute star that
attracts him, never able to reach dead center. Heating up under

repeated shocks, he first becomes dark red, then cherry, then white-hot, and spews out boiling globules and explodes once again, this time more violently, and his laughter becomes the fury of mad planets. And this chuckling fellow breaks something, he does.

Pataphysical laughter is the intense awareness of an absurd duality that gouges your eyes out. In this sense it is the only human expression of the identity of opposites (and, amazingly enough, it expresses this in a universal language). Or rather, it signifies the subject's headlong rush toward the opposed object, and at the same time the submission of this act of love to an inconceivable and cruelly-felt law of becoming—a law which prevents me from immediately attaining my totality, and according to which laughter is engendered in its dialectical progression:

I am Universal, I explode;
I am Specific, I contract;
I *become* Universal, I *laugh.*

And in turn, the act of becoming appears as the most tangible form of the absurd, and again I rebel against it by throwing out another burst of laughter, and so on indefinitely in this dialectical rhythm, which is the same as the panting of laughter in the thorax. I laugh for ever and ever, and this tumble downstairs never ends, for these laughs are my sobs, my hiccups, perpetuated by their own collision: the pataphysician's laugh, whether deep and deaf-mute or harrowing and on the surface, is also the only human expression of despair.

And faced with the faces that most resemble mine—those of other men—this despair folds onto itself in a final spasm; digging my nails into my palm, my fist clenches to crush a phantom egg whose yolk might nourish some hope of teaching, if only I could believe in it. No, I only wanted to say *what it was* for those who already knew, who had already laughed with this laughter, so that now they might know what I'm talking about.

You, who have settled into this mad sun, into this impossible burst of supreme lucidity, can hear Faustroll's great pataphysician's voice, and you can no longer believe that Jarry was

a joyful droll, nor that his Rabelaisian verve or Gallic tartness...
"*Ho hum! Ho hum!*" replies the profound echo of Marine bishop
Mendacious, and this outrageous reply is all such an insinua-
tion deserves.

The metaphysician has wormed his way into the world's pores
and into the evolution of phenomena, in the guise of the gnaw-
ing dialectic of bodies, which is the motor of revolutions. Now,
pataphysics *"is the science of that which is superinduced upon
metaphysics, either in itself or beyond itself, reaching as far beyond
metaphysics as the latter reaches beyond physics"* (Jarry). Dialectics
galvanized matter. Now it is pataphysics' turn to rush onto this
living body and consume it in its fire. We must expect the
imminent birth of a new age, to see a new force surge from
the extreme ramifications of matter. Devouring, gluttonous
thought, with respect for nothing, believing in and pledging
allegiance to no one, brutal with its own evidence in defiance
of all logic. This is the thought of the universal pataphysician
who will suddenly awaken in all men, breaking their backs with
a sneeze and laughing, and laughing, and disemboweling
the all-too-peaceful brain-cases with bursts of laughter. And
what a ruckus in the mouldy sarcophagi that house our
self-civilization!

I can only give brief indications here of the confusion in which
pataphysics will throw the various ways of thinking, acting and
feeling characteristic of lettuces—oops! I almost said "men."
Soon I hope to unveil, for example, my discovery of the pataphysics of love, and of a graphic method which enabled me to
plot the curve of "normal man," which is no mean joke, believe
me. For the moment, I will raise only a corner of the curtain
on these hilarious horrors:

Of pataphysics in general:
    "DEFINITION.–Pataphysics is the science of imaginary solu-
tions, which symbolically attributes the properties of objects,
described by their virtuality, to their lineaments" (Jarry). Thus
it is the opposite of physics as knowledge of the specific and
irreducible. Now, the existence of irreducibles is another facet
of my existence as a specific being: contradictory existence,
because at the same time I know myself to be part of the One.
Thus I will only know the irreducible by becoming One-the-

All. As such, we begin to see that pataphysics enshrouds a mystique, and reveals its perspectives in concrete form. To develop these several words would require hundreds of volumes. I nonetheless note Jarry's *revelation:* "It will examine the laws which govern exceptions, and WILL EXPLAIN THE UNIVERSE SUPPLEMENTARY TO THIS ONE." This "supplementary universe" is the inverse world where, according to primitive beliefs, the dead and the dreamers go—the hollow mold of this world. Put the world back into its mold and there is nothing left, neither hollows nor bumps, but a single whole. Consider the bowl of this pipe and all the characteristics that determine it. From a total understanding of this bowl we could deduce an understanding of the rest of the universe, by virtue of the principles of causality and reciprocal action. By the same token, remove this pipe-bowl from the world without changing anything else: you still think of it in its place, for it is impossible to deduce the bowl from an understanding of the universe minus the bowl. The two relations are symmetrical and reciprocal, and you can thus weigh the pipe-bowl against the rest of the universe. Letting this thought sink in will help you find your footing in pataphysics. To know x = to know (All-x).

Formal logic of pataphysics.

Pataphysics proceeds by means of *pataphysical sophisms.* The pataphysical sophism is a proposition which involves the non-conclusive modes of the syllogism, these modes becoming conclusive when one changes (in a way that, furthermore, imposes itself on the mind) the definition of certain terms. This change immediately entails a second stage of the same definitions, which again renders the employed modes of the syllogism non-conclusive, and so on indefinitely. Pataphysical knowledge concerns none other than the very law of this change. Pataphysical reasoning, instead of progressing according to the relations of extension between terms, possesses an actual and moving reality in the very comprehension of concepts. It passes through a dimension of reasoning that, for vulgar logic, is reduced to an immobile point. The reality of thought moves along a chain of absurdities, conforming to the great principle that *evidence can only manifest itself when clothed in absurdity.* Hence the comic appearance of pataphysical reasoning, which at the outset seems grotesque, then at second glance seems to contain a hidden meaning, then upon closer examination appears *decidedly* grotesque, then again more deeply meaningful, etc.—the evidence and the ridiculousness of a given proposition expanding and reinforcing each other *ad infinitum.*

Mathematical pataphysics.

Mathematical demonstrations conducted according to this logic will reveal an extraordinary richness. I need only take as witness the magnificent calculation of "the surface of God" at the end of *Faustroll.*

The pataphysics of Nature.

Pataphysics will make mockery of science, and be more educational. In my view, the creations of the pataphysical mind include:

The theory of natural selection ("this animal is so constituted because if it were not so constituted it could not exist": this type of demonstration forcefully posits the irreducible character of individual existence, and by a *reductio ad absurdum*—process proper to pataphysics—sketches the vicious circle of science all the while escaping it. In a nutshell: the irreducible is absurd; let us then reduce to the absurd in order to prove the obvious);

The discoveries of Jagadas Chander Bose on the nervous system of plants, which he arrived at through the simple contemplation of several species of vegetable life, inventing only *afterward* the apparatus which would allow Western scientists, provided they be of good will, to verify his discoveries;

The description of water by "Faustroll smaller than Faustroll" (*Faustroll,* IX); etc., etc.

Pataphysics in the industrial arts.

Leaving aside the countless inventions of the *five-hole button* type, the numerous peculiarities (due to pure whim) in fabricated objects are endless sources of pataphysical discussion. Just as pataphysics as knowledge is the inverse of physics and constitutes its opposite, it is also a powerful deterrent, as a mode of productive activity, against attempts to rationalize labor. All the forms governing the choice of a given decoration that no one will ever notice in the baggage rack of a railroad car, or of some detail on a random household object if nothing rational determines it; all those forces that remain dispersed in the general mass of producers: what wouldn't they be capable of one day, coordinated and made manifest? Such considerations give us a glimpse of a fantastic future for economic and social pataphysics.

More generally, for I can give only the most limited view of the fields open to devastation by this great laugh, the content of pataphysics is the "irreducible." Now, the irreducible is only such because one supposes an effort of reduction, of actual synthesis. The only effort of actual synthesis that I can know immediately is my own consciousness. Pataphysics, then, transposes knowledge from an abstract and universal understanding to a given present consciousness; that is, to a given determined power of synthesis, or to a given stage of digestion of the world by consciousness. The irreducible finally appears as the imprint of my current form on the world. —Thus pataphysics will provide, in the various domains of knowledge, activity, the arts and human societies, the measure of each man's descent into the rut of individual existence. And not only for the joy of measuring! For in this light, backbones will be rattled. Minds, bounced back and forth between laughter and sobs, between the parallel faces of sophisms, will be reflected indefinitely, and intense despair will leap upon them. We will have to find a way out.

Every man will experience the revelation of laughter, but let no one look to it for joy. At the point I have reached, the world's envelopes curl up like the fingers of a glove: the evident becomes absurd, light is a black veil, and a blazing sun sleeps, as my eyes do not.

Everyone will experience the revelation that any form is absurd as soon as it is taken seriously. In every human throat I hear the sound of a vocal mechanism, built up from the time of adolescence. I hear it say, with the mute resonance of the muzzle, underlining all speech, whether silent or aloud: "I am a man! I am a man!" To contemplate these constant, overwhelming attempts to be convinced of an arbitrary affirmation takes my breath away, and I am shaken from head to foot. "I am a man"? Why not say "I am Alphonse," or "I am a shopkeeper," or "con artist," or "mammal," or "philosopher," or "a proud animal"? And faced with the pretty sight of human actions, I am once again tormented by laughter. Faustroll snickers.

I think that anything we take seriously can be called a god. Anything can be taken seriously. If I adopt the attitude of the monster who does not laugh and if I gaze through his eyes over the infinite detail of forms, then everything is god — every point in space, every instant in a duration, every moment of consciousness is god. And thus we have the absurd and absolute multiplicy.

I now know that in the beginning, Chaos was ignited by an immense burst of laughter. In the beginning, Faustroll laughed the world.

The specific is absurd. In feverish states I have *seen* geometric figures and *inconceivable* movements. I have seen this with supreme evidence. Now I can see all things this way. The moment I understand a mathematical proposition, it seems divinely arbitrary in this light. As I said, the world turns before my eyes; my eyes turn back toward the night of the skull; the absurd is evident. I am Faustroll.

My look then shatters centuries of iron within me. I exist (therefore my ancestors must have existed) at the cost of this logic which, in an inhuman domain, seeks reasons to exist while twirling its moustache. At times, I am kind enough to provide it with some. But my laughter kills it.

Once we've reached a certain bend in the road, however, laughter is no longer enough. The sight of the arbitrary gives rise to man's fury, making revolt inevitable. This fearsome heritage of technicians wants me to believe that the world exists clearly, seriously. With a little sincerity, I no longer see clearly at all. A flower? Why does a flower exist? What does this mean? Why does any given thing exist? Oh no, the age of "why's" isn't over yet! They also tried to make me believe that there were several consciousnesses, a multitude of consciousnesses, that I was aware of *my*self while you were aware of *your*self. No: so long as this belief doesn't strike you as the most monstrous absurdity, you will not be able to take the first step toward yourselves. You will only be shadows.

The specific is revolting. But if I, who watch you take your revolt seriously, seek refuge beside Doctor Faustroll in his *Skiff* which is a riddle, I can still laugh. Is there nothing to be done, then? There is; for pataphysics is like nothing so much as a side-stepping: leave even that accidental but inevitable fury behind, and take it up again later as an iconoclastic force. It will be still another way of laughing, of negating and rejecting (as the first laugh renounced a part of the self, which was the World). And if, in negating everything, you should break something—hearts, hopes, palaces, statues, churches, intelligences, governments— remember, oh pataphysicians, under pain of turning back into serious boors, that this is not what you were looking for (in that case, it would be truly joyful!): that tears, blood and screams are the necessary effects of a desperate run on an endless track, of a momentum that negates the goal.

(1928; revised 1929.)

NADJA[1]

How predictable men are! *Nadja* gave the critics every opportunity to indulge in their depreciative efforts: they didn't pass
it up. The opportunity was too ripe, and André Breton had never
offered a better one. Finally they could apply their cliché
categories to a mind they considered one of today's most scandalous, and one of the most impervious to their stock expressions. *"Nadja,"* said these good men—and these good women,
perhaps—*"Nadja* is the marvelous. But we already know the
marvelous! We know it well! And love! And mysterious daily
encounters! Poetry, a glimpse of the unknown, Freud, liberty,
the life of the unconscious..." Yes indeed, the sorry riddles of
average French intelligence have done their job. Breton was not
afraid of their ilk; and what courage *still* to dare speak of mystery,
of love, of liberty! To write a book so that serious long-beards
could imagine they had recognized old stunted thoughts and
could congratulate the author on finally having written
something they could understand! "Finally," I can hear them
thinking, "a book by Breton that lets us show off our knowledge of psychology, and the tastes of our time, and the
tendencies of the new generation, and show that we're impar-
tial into the bargain! A remarkable literary event; Surrealism
has made something of itself after all, and..."—enough, already!
It would be easier to pardon the evil said of *Nadja* than these
degrading praises.

The marvelous, ah! yes, its eyes shine behind these pages,
these blinking eyelids. But I am afraid to speak of it, now that
virtually anyone can make it the decoration of his life. Dreams
have become wallpaper and mystery a carpet. Thereupon, one
indulges in the sorriest literary or psychological discussions,

1. By André Breton [English trans. by Richard Howard; New York,
1960].

gets carried away by juxtapositions and comparisons, and goes as far as to improvise metaphysics, which is one of the most repulsive ways of using speech. If I had time to demonstrate what I know—from having recognized it—or what I know that I do not know of the world and the mind, I could talk of the marvelous in general. Otherwise, I refuse. Of those coincidences which constantly burn out the eyes that dare to see them, I could say nothing that is not already contained in a given passage of *Nadja*, for example the one (page 59) in which Breton juxtaposes two facts whose absurd relation cannot be grasped immediately and about which, consequently, one can say no more.

I am trying to express myself amidst a confusion and misunderstanding, the sight of which is extremely grotesque. The marvelous of which I speak is the form human life necessarily takes as soon as I seek to escape it. You can see that I am quite far from understanding it, the way most do, as a charming veil thrown over the world to make us accept it, to console us for our boredom and our bondage. You have to observe mystery; open your eyes to this scandal, see what you have thus far refused to see. Or at least look at the reflection of the marvelous in other eyes, such as Nadja's or the eyes of those mediums who, if you truly want to *see*, will always spring up around you.

You will know what *Marvel* is, to use Breton's word; I cannot teach it to you. I can only repeat that it is not the sorry diversion of weak minds; it is not a way of making life "picturesque" (what is odious in the word is in keeping with the corresponding sentiment); it is not that easy consolation, so close to what theologians, who know what they're talking about, call *"delectatio morosa"*; it is not the multi-colored glass that you demanded from your glazier, oh Baudelaire, and with what sarcasm! For you, too, would have smashed these magic windows, as Marvel constantly breaks them, because it is not, oh no! it is not "the beautiful side of life"! These errors, these corruptions of meaning have finally made impossible the honest use of words such as "dream" or "attraction of mystery," which are now to the truly marvelous what bigotry is to love.

But it is still more difficult to speak of love. Around us we see hordes of sex-maniacs who would devote themselves wholeheartedly to so-called love. Their pitiful, impotent debaucheries go from animals all the way to God,[2] so much so that I could no longer write the word "mysticism" without adding a whole page of explanations. The con artists of the mind, with which literature is swarming, have stolen our dearest words. I believe they are extremely difficult to win back, as evidenced by the fact that the final pages of *Nadja*, which give the whole book its meaning, passed almost unnoticed. Perhaps no one heard behind them the eternal lines of Nerval's *Artemis*, which for me forms, along with "Lethe" from *Flowers of Evil*, the probable limit of what men will ever be able to say of their love. "The Thirteenth is coming back..." And how could it be otherwise, since eternal Love creates for itself its own various forms, and sets for itself the very goals that it will never attain? And I want to tell you right now, Sir, knowing full well what such a categorical proposition binds me to, that if for you the existence of consciousnesses distinct from your own goes without saying, free from either absurdity or inner turmoil, then you know nothing at all of love.

Here again I can only say: Love is not this, is not that. You will only know it by living with your eyes cruelly open, as Rimbaud demonstrated: agreeing to see everything without ever hoping to reach anything. And it is not a matter of calm contemplation, far from it! You will then see insanity, and miracles like those which, in *Nadja*, are strewn along André Breton's path. Walking with your face pierced by evidence, among those wearing the complicated blinders of our civilization, you will learn that in the kingdom of the blind even the clairvoyant is not king; that if, for example, you find a pair of eyes, magic mirrors, able to inform you about unknown aspects of yourself, they can be taken from you and broken. See what they did to Nadja, who was that for André Breton. There are insane asylums, as you know; there are also prisons, and police, and court juries;

2. Love is one, Love is that which loves — subject, not object. He for whom "loving love" means something is a stranger to love. By applying this rule, which has the value of a criterion, we could draw up a list of the main deviations from love, corresponding to just as many vices; we would easily find several all-too-familiar names to illustrate each of them (just think, for example, of the patriotic displacement of love). Such a task does not seem very useful at this time.

there is all the skillful brainwashing of a race of machine- or systems-builders. You will then feel, along with several rare humans, and with Breton, the acute necessity of joining, in a single act, poetry, love and revolt.

If these concerns do not come from a single source in you, I cannot believe you are sincere. These cares will then be a luxury of the civilized man, and will come under the same criticism that I addressed to the *"delectatio morosa."* If you write, for example, this could lead you to the psychological novel.[3] Breton's criticism of this kind of novel is of no small importance: the possibility of a work such as *Nadja* is in fact based on this criticism. Instead of giving in to continual disguises, to the incessant game of the novelist who dreams himself up and loves himself – by a kind of narcissism – through characters devoid of any sort of necessity,[4] Breton simply narrates himself. I use this last expression deliberately, precisely because of the alarming confusion it throws us into, which we must vanquish. *Breton* narrates *himself.* Who is narrated? Who is Breton? Where is the author? Here is the critical point at which I like to stay, and to which I would like to lead a few men. Those who are bothered by these questions have acquired only a rather narrow understanding of personality. André Breton does not express himself (which "me" would he choose to express?), does not exploit himself: he bares his soul – and frees his soul. For, by baring his soul, he directly participates in the universal. This is why *Nadja* is *necessary,* like a natural phenomenon. This is why the revelation, this blow to the heart or the groin, could not help but resound on the last page, that suddenly compelling cry: "Beauty will be CONVULSIVE or will not be at all."

(1928.)

3. All psychology, if it is only psychology – that is, claiming the title of discursive science – is the mark of an inability to realize in oneself the absolute idealism which is a necessary moment of thought.

4. This quality of immediately-thought necessity is the true beauty of a work, and its only reason – or excuse – for being.

ON THE ATTITUDE OF CRITICISM
WITH RESPECT TO POETRY[1]

(This rapid sketch claims nothing less than to establish the foundations of a criticism applicable to poetry. The task was indispensible. It is not enough. The condemning judgment it passes on the majority of so-called critics and on our most respected contemporaries' ways of living and thinking must be complemented by concrete attacks. But I am sure that those who surround me, those with whom I lead this struggle, will not forget these poisoned darts. Today I will show them the art of taking aim. I add that if my thought, in its abstract form, were understood by the defenders of law and order, I would run far less risk of their outrage by spitting in their faces.)

I am, first of all, not entirely sure that a book such as Rolland de Renéville's *Rimbaud the Seer* is what common language would call a work of criticism. But I prefer to show charity toward common language by slightly broadening the meaning of this word, so as to pronounce it other than with a grimace of disgust. Today, when a living word can become essential only by surrounding itself with the most extreme rigor, amidst the literary swarm of practical recipes thanks to which anyone possessing no more than an agile pen can, by shaking a few cold corpses, imitate a flood of revelations; today, when the Verb is prostituted; when Beauty is sold to the rabble of brush or pen; when Truth is sold to the rabble of science who build machines to deaden the mind and destroy; when Good is sold to legislative and law-enforcement rabble; when the Spirit is sold to ecclesiastical rabble—today, simply to justify an undertaking is already to glorify it.

This justification of a work cannot simply be vague approval. Rather, it must be a strict demonstration of the work's internal and external necessity. To *justify* the work is to establish that it is *legitimately* placed among external things precisely where it must be, and that internally all of its parts are *legitimately* placed

---

1. And exemplarily on *Rimbaud the Seer* [Rimbaud le voyant] by A. Rolland de Renéville.

27

one in relation to the others as they must be. It is to prove that the work is necessary because it is determined in its organic nature, from without and from within. I see now that to call this effort "criticism," in the true philosophical sense of the word, is not an abuse of language, and that the ones who are wrong are those who bestow this name on the most sterile verbiage. I said that simply to justify a work was to glorify it: but don't you see that, after a severe critical examination conducted in the manner described, only a single drop of pure water would remain out of the whole literary sea—that realm of whim most vain in which all the facile minds of this century swim their parasitic stroke? Only a single drop of pure water, indeed, but intensely swollen with the Flood!

Criticism must mercilessly destroy every useless work; that which is not necessary is bad. And, as a critic of criticism, I want to be just as merciless. The better to show the rules by which a work of criticism will be judged, I will add to my definition the example of *Rimbaud the Seer*, as one of the few books capable of withstanding such a test.

Here the object of criticism is a poet, and what a shining star! Now, all that we've said about criticism so far takes on a particularly blinding and, for many, irritating and troubling character as soon as Poetry is brought into play. I remind you that the task is to show luminously that the poet wrote a necessary corpus of work, bound by a rigorous determinism to the whole of the contemporary world, and supported by a law just as perfectly inflexible, uniting each part to the whole. This demonstration is the only one capable of proving the work's value, an absolute value which resides in the poet's freedom. This freedom, the source of all values, is (as Spinoza understands it, and any other meaning is impossible) that of the man who frees himself by thinking of himself as determined by universal will. The poet's thought is a law of Nature, and there is no beauty other than that immediate, miraculously sensual appearance of the universal and necessary in the particular object that they call into being.[2] Thus one cannot talk about a

---

2. I ask the reader, in passing and as an example, to ponder the reasons that make me write "call into being" and not "create," and more generally a certain word loaded with meaning and not some other with apparently the same signification. The conciseness of this essay

poet without setting in motion not only an aesthetic, but also a metaphysic and an ethic.

First, I wish to enumerate the different possible kinds of criticism, and to define the legitimate one by progressive elimination of the others. I am leaving out another way of talking about poets: the lyrical way. The words of one poet can become, for another who receives them and vibrates with their shocks, an object of disturbance, stupor or enthusiasm; a dazzling impulse stronger than the knots of laziness, sleep or routine, or the exalting star of a revelation demanding a new interpreter. It can give rise to a new poem in which the rhythms of the first creator's breath, heart and mind are composed with the resonances proper to the second. But although a powerful critical thought can become part of it, a work such as Mallarmé's "A Tomb for Edgar Poe" is not criticism. It goes without saying that I neither judge it nor simply explain it; no, first I let it shake my spine as would the hand of a ghost gloved with, and guiding, a hand of living flesh.

(But I am extremely suspicious of that kind of lyrical paraphrasing of the poem—which sometimes passes itself off as criticism—favored these days by the popularization and decline of Surrealist writing and become a process "within everyone's reach." The transformation of this miraculous invention into a literary formula has allowed several obscure but somewhat flexible opportunists of the mind to ape poetry and drool around true poets streams of verse full of false marvels and facile bursts of imagery. And thanks to the ambiguity of this means of expression, which is by turns the writer's instrument and his master, they are allowed to speak without meaning, because they will be pardoned and their drool called "rivers of symbols...deep...full of intentions hidden under the metaphors." Thus they can risk the worst stupidities because others will forgive them in the name of sacred automatism, telling us: "These beauties cannot be understood, you must feel them, or else you lack any poetic sense, my dear sir." To my mind,

forces me to reduce the number of easy expressions to the minimum, and to use a term only in its most precise and powerful meaning—no doubt despite several errors or omissions, almost as unimportant as they are unavoidable.

there is no better way to insult such a poet, who turns me away sobbing like a bottle spilling water, than to indulge in similar exercises of the pen under the guise of praise.)

The critics themselves fall into two major categories. The first ones always judge the poet on the unspoken assumption that he freely wrote his work, choosing one expression over another according to aesthetic, moral or logical principles: the same principles that help the critic judge the poem. The second ones try to explain or justify the work by showing it to be clearly determined. What I have said of criticism in general condemns the former. They judge the poem according to their own criteria, which they arbitrarily ascribe to the poet. Aesthetic prejudices: "how beautiful *The Drunken Boat* is! what mastery of rhythm and vocabulary! what a skillful handling of sounds!..." Or: "how ugly the *Illuminations* are! what lack of composition! what misrecognition of real beauty!..." There you have two opinions (and unfortunately not the most idiotic), one just as sadly foolish as the other. Logical prejudices, ignoble if they serve to condemn the poet in the name of "clarity," of "good sense" (and by what a corruption of the value of these words); still more disgusting if they are put forward as glorifications. Moral prejudices, the most repulsive, if they condemn Rimbaud for respecting neither family, country, God nor (horrors!) himself, and even more so if they praise him with filthy arguments such as: "he depicts evil to purify himself, the better to incite us to do good...," etc. These useless chatterers, idiots when they attack, odious when they defend, presuming free will on the part of the poet, dress that caricature of freedom in all the baseness, flaws and tics of their own minds. For their judgments to be justified, they should be based on sure principles, identical for the critic judging and the poet being judged; but identical they will surely never be unless they are founded in the universal and are, consequently, principles of determination. But then the critic would be of the second type, a seeker of poetic necessity.

Among the latter, we must distinguish three classes. Certain critics wish to establish the poem's external necessity. Others, its internal necessity. The last, finally, seek to determine the poem from within and from without. Mr. Taine is the paragon of the first type. He would have said, roughly, something like: "Rimbaud was born in an austere region with a harsh climate to an ill-tempered mother, and lived in troubled times; that is why he wrote 'Paris Repopulated,' which is austere, harsh and ill-tempered, and which reflects troubled times." There has been no lack of such explanations. In this vein, J.M. Carré sees in Rimbaud's double life the dual hereditary influence of his father and his mother.

And still no critic has held to a rigorous sytem of materialist criticism of Rimbaud. Some could perhaps expect a lot from strict adherence to this method. But it would only give us the poet's corpse. Materialism—I mean vulgar materialism—proposes only matter, as the word itself says. It could, given a poem by Rimbaud, suspend it from a chain of causes. But the chain breaks at the poem, and if the poem had been otherwise, so the chain would have been otherwise; for it is constructed after the fact, it links only past facts, it is on the side of death. The *a posteriori* reconstruction of a causal link leading up to a poem is unable to determine it, however paradoxical this may be. Such an attempt is false and perfectly useless, and I have difficulty seeing what designs those who undertake it are pursuing. I prefer not to go into this for the moment, and to leave the sad handlers of musty old bones to their sterile games, so long as they do not take advantage of the semblance of rigorous science to treacherously dirty a man and begin, in insidious medical studies, condemning him in the name of moral health.

A second way is to seek the poem's determination within itself, its Meaning: no longer in its matter, but in its idea. Now, no idea is real unless active in a mind. The essence of the poem is the poet's thought in its pure unity, which, penetrating and animating the multiple language, gives the words their meaning. This creative act, free by origin, imposes its law on the verbal chaos presented by the mechanism of the voice or writing. The poem's necessity will thus be proven if the critic recognizes the poet's thought as being in itself identical to his own and to universal thought speaking through a particular organ. In other words, and without returning to that supreme source, as the scientist seeks the immutable in the changeable and by this inquiry formulates laws, so in the moving diversity of words the critic will pursue the identical. Now, to seek the law that imitates the scattered members of a word is to work toward the constitution of a doctrine. This task cannot be performed without an original schema, an anticipation of the doctrine, a dogma. Criticism will thus establish the internal necessity of a work by relating the author's thought to a pre-conceived doctrine.

But from this moment on, the most arbitary choice of dogma threatens to be made. For the distinctive feature of an *a priori* dogma is its ability to feed on any experience. Anything can serve as its body, for the dogma's transcendental character absolutely rejects all pure determination of its form and of the *a posteriori* elements that will embody it. We see here that the word criticism more than ever takes on the sense of a Kantian critique, and that the *Critique of Pure Reason* pulls the rug out from under Mr. Paul Claudel. The same transcendental character, which confers upon the dogma its respectable quality (as opposed to miserable matter), causes the search for the determining dogma of the poem to quickly become illustrative of the dogma through the poem. And in fact, the respectable dogma *par excellence*, which wants to be respected and to dominate miserable matter, is the Christian dogma. The God of the Jews, on the whole, has remained just as much that of the Christians as that of the Muslims: he is eminently the summary of all things transcendental. The rigorous dualism of Christian doctrine was meant to allow this abstract Eternal to feed, while deprecating all food. The gaping mouth covered by the mask of the sad ambassador, in his gluttony of a spiritual puppet that aspires to life and is hungry for blood, did not respect, could not have respected Arthur Rimbaud.*

To summarize: criticism founded on principles or rules of taste, whether clearly thought or simply felt, is false. Materialist criticism and ordinary dogmatic criticism are false, for matter separated from the idea is nothing, as is the idea separated from matter. And as they are not real, we can find the principle of necessity that will justify the work in neither one nor the other.

I have shown that dogmatic criticism becomes blameworthy as soon as one must choose a dogma, that is, as it always hap-

*Paul Claudel, 20th-century poet and noted French diplomat, ascribed his devout Catholicism to a reading of Rimbaud.

pens, as soon as one gives in to the arbitrary. But even if we should find a necessary dogma, implying in itself its own manifestation in the diversity of the word, such a dogma would stop being a transcendental principle, and would immediately put us in the heart of reality, at the point of impact between the poetic sunbeam and the chaotic mother-sea of words, in the beating heart of the poem. This would be the sole doctrine capable of demonstrating the necessity of such a word, and its application to criticism would be the only legitimate one. This doctrine is necessary, hence possible; it follows that we can and must define it and constitute it explicitly.

Now, going back through the given conditions toward the supreme principle to be established, we find ourselves face to face with a poetic Fire, whose subtle splendor permeates all true poetry, swells the words of prophets and the revelations of the illuminated, expresses itself in the awesome explosives which are the *Vedas,* the books of Lao-tse, the *Cabbala,* and the endless reservoirs of gasoline that were built around them. Every poet we love, every poet who rattles us from stomach to throat, who steals our breath away, has been a mouthpiece for this single Doctrine.

It is in view of this Doctrine that Rolland de Renéville retraces the shining trajectory followed by Rimbaud in the sky of miraculous fate. He does not make Rimbaud's work simply an illustration of the doctrine; he does not make the doctrine simply a plausible hypothesis to explain the life and works of Rimbaud. But through the work he founds the doctrine and through the doctrine he founds the work.

I will not try to summarize the Doctrine here: you can read Renéville's own exposé. This true science is idealistic in that it starts from the only real, materialistic Idea, going essentially in the same direction (in that it penetrates its intimate substantial nature), in the same sense as Rimbaud when he prophesied: "This century will be materialistic." By what I've written, I hope to help the reader of *Rimbaud the Seer* to notice how the Doctrine of matter alone permits Renéville to render the poet's metaphysical aspect, his scandalous aspect, the flesh-and-blood thinker who meditates in the world the way a volcano erupts. This is real thought that frightens the rooted man, the liberal bourgeois for whom a person can have whatever opinions he or she likes on supreme reality: "For, after all, speculation is a matter for metaphysicians, very quiet and intelligent men who will not trouble either the social order or the other's peace by the movement of their thought; whether one is dualist or monist, idealist or materialist, realist or nominalist, free unto himself, we are tolerant—and so what? The world will not change for so little; thought is something light, winged, tenuous, immaterial, and..." No! the path of thought is lead, living it moves mountains and fires revolvers, and because that quiet man is a monist and not a dualist, or a realist and not a nominalist, he is going to kill you.

Having said that criticsm, in order to justify itself, must strictly justify poetry, I know that I will be asked time and again: but does poetry need justification? Why attempt to mediate the determination of an object whose necessity is immediately felt? Does anyone—author, reader or poet—gain anything from the fact that *Rimbaud the Seer* was written?

I will answer that such a work is useful to the author and perhaps to several readers, and sometimes even to the poet. But this is only true of a work conforming to the definition I've given of legitimate criticism. Thus I cannot prove what I have just put forth any better than by leaning on the predominant doctrine of Renéville's book, as on one of the clearest forms of the single Doctrine. This Doctrine, whose purest aspect shines in the Aryan East, has been transmitted to the West, from the heart of the wise centuries up to ours, by three paths. The first is the philosophical path, along which pure teaching is still luminous in the Ephesian and Eleatic Dialectics, as well as the Platonic. But this teaching declines when it adapts to the necessities of techniques of societal organization and machine-building, only to founder in pragmatics after passing through Hegelian Dialectics—in itself treacherous when it stoops to the point of claiming to justify imperialist order—and the Dialectics of Hamelin, which has almost totally abandoned its splendid origins to become no more than a logic. The second path, that of the occult traditions, is initiatory. The various schools of cabbalists, hermeticists, alchemists and astrologers it engenders certainly desire to convey the totality of primitive systems to each other. Still, this path is not free of betrayals; and I am alluding not only to the charades of modern Freemasonry (oh, Hiram!), but especially to the far more terrible successes of certain corruptions of the initiatory chapels: the Churches. The poetic path is the third. This luminous Father of true knowledge, that of the initiates, is also that of poets, of true poets who are bound together by the radiant bond of a mysterious kinship.[3] Now, poetry also betrayed this bond by coming to the West, by becoming Art.

Whoever, in this century, has worth in my eyes is someone who struggles to retrace these currents, either in full consciousness of all three or, obscurely, of one or two of them. But the three are essentially inseparable; they represent three moments of thought. That is why such a man, my friend, is necessarily the enemy of the three great Betrayals: enemy of Philosophical Betrayal and of the discursive science of Western legislators and technicians; enemy of the Betrayal of Mysticism, of religion and of the societies it supports with its hypocritical ideologies; enemy of Poetric Betrayal and of the cadaver-art which false souls seek to animate with an illusory life.

Each one, according to its means, will rise more specifically against one or the other of these enemies. But it is good to organize the struggle and—this is the first point I wanted to prove—he who thinks about a poet can only win by rediscovering in himself the verbal system which binds poetic revolution to philosophical and mystical revolution: going back to the source, he sees the triple current of his Revolt, he contemplates its necessity, submits to it and becomes a stronger agent of revolt. Secondly, his word, when heard by someone who only weakly feels one of the three currents in his head, heart or gut, can help arouse awareness of the two others, and thus give rise (I know that this may apply to only one among a crowd of readers) to a new agent of the threefold Revolt.

3. The unity of these three traditions means that it matters little to me whether a certain poet was initiated into a certain mystery or knew a certain philosophy; it is *obvious* that poetic discoveries must be in accordance with the discoveries of occultism. Whether or not Rimbaud read books on the Cabbala and magic is of strictly documentary interest in Renéville's book—moving, certainly, but not essential. I would almost prefer this fact to be false, so that certain people would not be led to believe that Rimbaud had "learned" his revelations in books.

I have justified André Rolland de Renéville's book as an effort to explicate what the poetic sense immediately grasps: the conjunction of the free Verb (itself being determined by the formal field of words) with the inflexible docility—a conjunction that created Rimbaud, among other poets. Each one can, for the details, take up this justification according to the dialectic I have sketched. Let him read *Rimbaud the Seer* as one of the best examples of the only kind of criticism that can legitimately be applied to a poet. Furthermore, I'm not claiming that legitimate criticism cannot take very different forms, manifest its doctrine in altogether different terms; whether its approach falls under the aegis of the *Vedas*, the *Cabbala*, Plato, Spinoza or Hegel, or whether it leaves the theoretical aspect of the doctrine simply understood, its validity can still be proven by means of the present thesis, which is schematically summarized as follows:

(1929.)

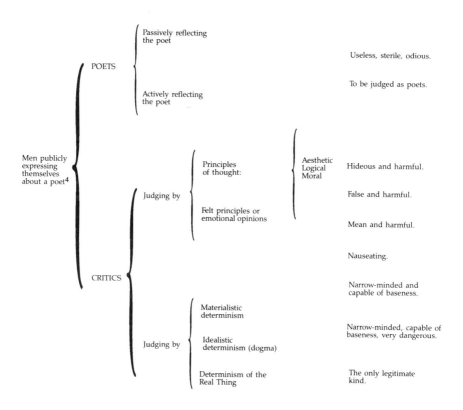

4. Of course, there is probably no critic who can be strictly enclosed in one category or another. It is the same each time a classification is made. We will always find that a critic expresses himself according to both emotional tendencies and a certain dogma, or to both an aesthetic and a physiological given, etc. I will be satisfied with merely proposing a schema, among other possible ones, *so that afterward it may be used.*

NERVAL THE NYCTALOPE

to Robert Meyrat

What is night for all beings is the time of
awakening for the self-controlled; and the time
of awakening for all beings is night for the
introspective sage.

Bhagavad Gita, II, 69.

So I was observed! I was not alone in this world—this world
that I could have thought a product of my imagination! this
precious asylum for those disgusted with life, for social
impotents, this easy refuge for "escapists," as they say! But I
laugh out loud when I hear this language. Yes, of course I knew,
I have always known that this world was populated, that there
were crowds out there, and that an enormous sarcastic eye
watched over it; a sun that does not light, but sees, contrary to
the blind and shining daytime sun. I knew that an eye laughed
silently, wide open on this nocturnal domain which we like to
think of as whim and perfect solitude. I still know it, it's true,
but each time I re-read *Aurelia*—and this is saying a lot—a new
shock of certainty in the pit of my stomach opens the eye in
my heart: so I was observed! I was not alone in this world!
Because Nerval has been there, because he describes for me
what I saw there, often even what I lived through there.

My oldest and richest memories, from the very first years of
my life, are memories of dreams. Since then, in certain periods,
it is always into the same Country that my sleep has led me,
once I've crossed the intermediate region of light dreams (true
or distorted reflections of events and concerns from my waking
state, mimed representations of discomforts or appetites). It is
the same Country I recognize without a doubt: the same City,
the same Countryside, the same Outskirts, the same Palace,
with its Arsenal, its two Theaters, its Museums; I could draw
a fairly precise map. But especially the life that one leads

there; the drama or comedy that eternally unfolds; the precise and invariable meaning that certain gestures acquire, obeying strict symbolic laws; the seriousness and fated nature accorded a given determined act—all of this only expresses that truth to which I bear witness: the world of the Dream. And *by "world" I mean a particular way of knowing through sensitive intuition what I affirm to be not myself;* in other words, in the final account, *a determined condition of my consciousness* considered as a synthesis of representations. This world is universal: I mean both common, *a priori,* to every human mind, and constituting a universe, or rather a facet of the Universe. Or again, it is directed by universal necessity. It is not the privileged refuge of chance, contingency or whim banished from the waking world; it is not the shelter of irresponsibility, since the slightest gesture in this dream-life can seriously implicate the dreamer, in his phantom existence and at times in his physical existence.

To avoid having all this be seen as sweet daydreams, or as a vague taste for mystery and facile ramblings on the supernatural, I will immediately tell of my experience and give the formula that will allow anyone who has the courage to attempt an experimental verification. It was in a real world that, several years ago, I held nocturnal meetings with my friend Robert Meyrat. No need to scale the fence of the family home in order to escape through the deserted streets of a provincial town and enjoy nights full of marvelous adventures. Here is the process that I had discovered for leaving my body (I have since learned that occult science has known this since antiquity); I lay down at night like everyone else and, carefully relaxing all of my muscles, making sure that each one was completely and totally abandoned unto itself, I breathed long and deeply, in a regular rhythm, until my body was no more than a foreign, paralyzed mass. I then imagined that I rose from bed and got dressed, but—and it is for this essential point that I require uncommon courage and powers of attention from all who would imitate me—I imagined each movement in its slightest detail, and with such precision that I had to imagine the action of putting on a slipper in exactly the same amount of time it would have taken me to put it on in bodily life. I admit, furthermore, that sometimes I had to spend a week in vain attempts each night before merely being able to sit up on the edge of my bed, and that the fatigue caused by such exercises often forced me to interrupt them for long periods of time. If I had the energy to continue, the moment came, more or less quickly, when I was *launched*. Seen from outside, I was asleep. But in reality I was wandering effortlessly, even with the desperate ease that those who remember dying know so well. I walked and, immobile, I saw myself walking at the same time, in completely unfamiliar neighborhoods, with Meyrat beside me. The next day, in broad daylight, we rejoined Gilbert-Lecomte and Vailland, and told them of our walk.

I would be very disturbed by someone's laughter at this narrative. To laugh at *that*, at that game of death which we had all resolved to play day and night, awake or asleep; laugh at that drama which unfolded in our dreams, and which perhaps has not counted its last victim! Let them first try my little formula. Robert Meyrat haunted our sleep. For him, no friendship was possible without these nocturnal meetings, or at least without the visits he paid to each of us without respite, anxious to know if we would only welcome him, capable – I write this slowly, deliberately, weighing my words – of dying the very next day if one evening he had found us resolutely closed, if his ghost had arrived only to rebound off our inert mummies, making it return too quickly, with too brutal a shock on his heart, to the form of his sleeper's skin. (And yet, one day, what had happened? You never told us if, one after the other, we had all refused you welcome; nor what accident had occurred – in what intersection of nightmares? – so that you suddenly stopped frightening young people like yourself, stopped appearing before them with bloody fangs. Did you lack your vampire's food – once more, I weigh my words – and from lack of this food, could you have become human? The drama that decided our absurd and incomprehensible separation had to play itself out in that world which was so familiar to you – is it still?)
I have perhaps faltered, I admit, and sometimes lost awareness of our tasks, our struggles in that country where you never joined me again. I followed Gérard de Nerval there. I saw through his eyes as I had seen through my own: the same sights. Do you remember the night in the park when you blew my brains out? I was sure of *leaving* and I had taken my departure from the world with an ease that astonished me. A recurring vision from my dreams surged from the chiming of the last bells,

during the last secular instant of waiting. It showed immense marble stairs leading up a hill with its peak in splendor. Often strange sculpted rocks or reptile-plants, or other cunning games of a mutant Nature had prevented my climb. This time I was sure to succeed! The radiant stairway led all the way to the gigantic ceiling of light vaulted into a world, but free and shining! Do you remember how I rolled on the ground when I realized you had fooled me, that it was only a false departure? I would even forgive you a "good joke," for I recognized that "it was, alas, not yet time."

About three years later, what a jolt I received upon reading *Aurelia* for the first time: Nerval knew the country of long trials; he knew the Castle with its countless hallways, cut by endless stairways. Could I ever make anyone understand the mad certainty that caused me to recognize the blood of my blood in such simple descriptions:

"...a kind of inn with immense stairways, full of busy travelers";

"...I lost my way several times in long corridors..."?

And how can I prove that the silent word addressed to me in the vision—that I took for my last—of the stairway; how, when I am more certain of it than of the beating of my own heart, when I have blood in my eyes from the brutal evidence, how can I prove that it is the same word that Nerval heard? "I was" (he says, but it is just as much I who speak) "in a tower, deep into the ground and so high into the sky that all my existence seemed destined to be spent climbing and descending..." — Yes: "She said to me" (*She* said to *me*! "the goddess of *my* dreams..."!): *"The ordeal you have undergone is coming to an end; the endless stairways which wore you out so going up and down were the bonds of old illusions that hindered your thought."*

It was perhaps three years after *that*. No doubt I have yet to write many pages in my life which will encircle me, which will turn and tighten closer and closer around the central simplicity of my naked reality. But never, oh no! never will any book by my hand have the exact color of my blood, never will any book be so truly mine as *Aurelia*.

Only experience will teach me if my personal testimony can pass for anything other than literature or convince several readers of the reality of such experiments. Before citing other

authorities, I nonetheless insist on declaring once more that
I have seen, as Nerval saw:

The *Palace* full of stairways and corridors in which the Same awaits us, in which I have not finished wandering, lost, and for how many centuries to come?

The *Tower,* the *Castle* and the *Mysterious City* of the dead.[1]

I have seen the sunless Country. And when I read ın *Aurelıa:* "Everyone knows that in dreams we never see the sun, although

1. Re-read the description of this City in *Aurelia;* I could confirm many details. But you can imagine what anguish I felt reading it for the first time, if you know that long before, toward the end of August 1925, Roger Vailland received two letters, containing these excerpts:

One was from Robert Meyrat, and came from a beach on the English Channel: *"We were...*quite literally *cloistered in an immutably nocturnal city filled with roofs of naked tile, endlessly living impotent reveries.* Now, *escape was decided upon,* and Daumal, you, Gilbert-Lecomte and I crept catlike along *the tile rooftops and the gutters,* escaping from the cops lying in wait near the streetlamps. Finally, reunited in a large garden with bushy clumps of geraniums. At last we were going to escape from the influence. You wanted to pick tall, white, strong-scented flowers for me. Perhaps they were *arums. You handed me the long white corolla,* while making a face. Then *the Women* appeared *and we remained prisoners, because* you wanted to give me flowers."

The other letter was from me and came from Reims: "Last night I was on La Nouvelle—a small island a little larger than Mont Saint-Michel and of the same form—with H... and L...; *we were in prison. We escaped* as easily as could be and I resolved to swim to Europe. I climbed to the highest point and, knowing that I had to go due West, looked at the setting sun—*rooftops ad infinitum, rooftops piled up at random; as far as the eye could see, the city flowed interminably in cataracts of houses.* All three of us descended toward the Eastern bank, following a street that looked like Place Pigalle (perhaps at that moment Gilbert-Lecomte was there)... From the basket I was carrying protruded a stick which was gold with brown mottling, bent in half. Noticing that it was a snake, I threw it on the ground; it crawled quickly for several yards, then began to fly. *A young girl* made a monkey dance at the end of a string. *H... immediately began to flirt with her. Once again I saw the endless city, and,* with great pains, transformed it to give it the exact appearance of my room. Thereupon I peacefully awoke. I'm sure this dream is prophetic, but I can't interpret it yet."

I now underline the explicit coincidences and, much more important, the enunciations of the Drama that those who *have really lived there* will understand.

we often perceive a much stronger light. Objects and bodies illuminate themselves..." I know that I must consider an imposter whoever, claiming to have explored Dreams, is not violently struck in his body and soul by the obvious universal value of this law, which is so much greater than any physical law. The fact that light, in the dream, emanates from every form, whereas in the waking state it originates in a transcendental light-source (so to speak) which is separated from the forms left to their own night, perfectly expresses (I leave this to be meditated, and may you make the most of this rare opportunity!) just how differently we conceive of things (the same things) in the dream and the waking state.

And when I read: "I felt myself slip as on a taut wire of infinite length," I know very well that this wire is an invisible vein of space, rigid as steel, more similar to the space that separates two very close telegraph wires than to the wires themselves, an inflexible direction of anguish that can only be perceived by an organ located near the throat. On my throat I slipped along these wires in my childhood dreams, and several days later I came down with an angina. (I know that this immediately provides a *physiological explanation* (!) *of the phenomenon.* But I do not accept this reversal of cause and effect, when the congestion of the throat area caused by a rush of blood from the excessive attention that the violent emotion of my dream made me concentrate on that part of my body sufficiently explains the increased susceptibility of the mucous membranes in the back of my mouth to pathogenic microbes always floating around the atmosphere.)

And this! "A kind of mysterious choir reached my ears; children's voices repeated in unison: *Christe! Christe! Christe!...* I thought that someone had gathered a large number of children in the neighboring church (Notre-Dame-des-Victoires) to invoke Christ." How many times have I heard these childlike chants before falling asleep—and their distress! I understand it now, because what they were celebrating was the night of the dead, what they were invoking was a hopeless abyss. "'But Christ is no more!' I said to myself. 'And they do not know it yet!'"

And the "Serpent that surrounds the Earth": six years ago, in broad daylight, in the middle of the street, I saw its head, the head of the Naja, rise with terrifying slowness above the rooftops, gradually eating and replacing the sun, to become the "Black Sun."

And that drama always begun anew! the presence of that Double who acts in your name, without your being able to do anything about it, and steals the fire from your life; the impotence of your anger! I remember that in the land of the dead, where I spent several seconds (no doubt) of a dream—seconds which were months—I, too, upon arrival, had wanted to be angry. I didn't know it yet, but the maddening ease of the slightest movement (I ripped a monumental oak door from its hinges as if it were a feather), the fatally ironic smile of the other dead men, and the implacable softness of the master's face had already disarmed me. Nerval, how many men other than yourself know what sobs must be stifled when you say that simple sentence: "Those around me seemed to be laughing at my impotence"?

I still have many witnesses to call upon. Gilbert-Lecomte, first of all, to whom few of my experiments are unknown. We quickly recognized each other, upon our human meeting, by stirring some of the age-old masses of our common memories: he knows the Castle with its corridors, the cobblestones of the City of the Dead, and especially what light—light without sun, of course—reigns there. (Before hearing others speak about it, I called it "pearled light"; I have since learned that it was "astral light.") He knows the Stairways and the Serpent, the children's choirs and the throat-piercing astral beams...

But there would be no end to the references I could give. I would have to quote every poet I love.

The Egyptian *Book of the Dead,* the sacred books of India, the *Zohar,* occultism, folklore and the "primitive mind" contain an extraordinarily far-reaching and coherent science of the dream world (or astral world), and in these texts I find perfect correspondences to each vision, to each of Nerval's experiences. I hold back the pen that would like to drag me along for a Swedenborgian number of pages, and I cite somewhat at random:

Again, those *pathways to astral space,* one pathway being the *Ray* that was to lead Nerval to the *Star;* they correspond, in the microcosm, to the *nadis,* astral arteries of the Hindus. "...The Self is the origin of a hundred and one paths; there are a hundred of them in each and, in each of the latter, one thousand times seventy-two ramifications. In each, penetrating life circulates. By the hundred-and-first, ascendant life leads to the pure abode when it rises purely, etc."[2]

The point on the nape of the neck to which Nerval applies a talisman, explaining his precaution thus: "This point was the one at which the soul would be liable to leave the body when a certain ray, come from the star I had seen the night before, coincided relative to me with its zenith." This point is analogous to the "hole of Brahma," passage of the "hundred-and-first path" or "sun's ray" (cf. *Chandogya Upanishad*, VIII, 6, 5; *Aitareya Upanishad*, I, 3, 12; etc.).

The underground kingdom, from universal tradition (*Aurelia*, passim; cf. the Tibetan legends concerning the *Agarttha*).[3]

The elementals: Divas, Peris, Water Sprites, Salamanders, Afreets (these latter corresponding to the Gnomes of the cabbalists).[4]

The bird through whose voice the ancestor spoke. It is hardly necessary here for me to underline the obvious similarity to primitive totemism. Furthermore, Nerval's revelations on the condition of the dead in the "astral," that is, on the life of the double, correspond exactly to primitive eschatologies (cf. Lévy-Bruhl), to that of the Egyptians and to what I have seen myself.

The harmony of the spheres (which is not, we must realize, a

2. *Prashna Upanishad*, III, 6, 7.—Telling of his execution through the medium of Victor Hugo's pedestal table, André Chenier said, "Light flows through my transparent veins." (Gustave Simon, *Les Tables tournantes de Jersey* [The seance tables of Jersey]; Paris, 1927.)

3. CF. Saint-Yves d'Alveydre, *La Mission de L'Inde* [India's mission].—F. Ossendowsky, *Bêtes, hommes et dieux* [Beasts, men and gods].—René Guénon, *Le Roi du monde* [The king of the world].

4. It is remarkable that Nerval is much closer to Hindu tradition here than to any other form of occult tradition. The majority of occultists, in fact, speak only of four elements: air, water, fire and earth, inhabited by Sylphs (Fairies, Peris), Water Sprites, Salamanders and Gnomes. The Hindus are practically alone in bringing in a fifth element, ether; and the *Divas* Nerval speaks of are certainly the *Devas*, the "shining ones," over whom reigns Indra—Lord, in fact, of the Ether. I must add that to each of these elements correspond *elementary essences* or *rudiments (tanmatras),* which are their *a priori* determinations—in other words, what they are in themselves when all of their accidental characteristics have been negated. Now, Nerval says: "Each time one of these creatures died, it was immediately reborn in a more beautiful form and sang to the glory of the gods."

simple figure of rhetoric), *the winged Lama*, Kheroubim of vital fire penetrating inert matter (the couple fire-water, or father-mother, or Iod-He, or phallus-cteis, or sulfur-mercury, etc., is universally known to be the motor and the dialectical knot of creation in all the occult traditions), *the hinge of world history,*[5] *the Pact of the Elohims, the division of the world, the monstrous genesis, the evolution of races, the cursed Necromancers, the final Pardon granted the Serpent which encircles the Earth,* whose sections, "separated by iron...are joined together in a hideous kiss glued by men's blood"; the terrible lucidity of this discovery that each man must make: "an error had slipped, I felt, into the general continuation of numbers," the *Madmen who reform the Cosmos, the unknown metals*[6]...but I would have to copy all of *Aurelia* from beginning to end. I only want you to know what should nonetheless be patently obvious: that nothing in this book is accidental or fanciful, that whim has no place in it, and that each statement, each description, each narrative of Nerval's can be found a thousand times over in the enormous knowledge of the initiates and seers throughout the ages. And it would be useless to "explain" Nerval's dreams by his readings and his vast knowledge, acquired from the Freemasons, the *Cabbala,* Hermeticism, Pythagorism, magic, the theosophies and cosmogonies of India, Persia and Chaldea, from astrology, Germanic legend, etc. It was because the essence of that science was inscribed, planted between his eyes, that all his life he was possessed by the need to seek out its manifestations. Otherwise, we could not explain why it dominated his dreams so dramatically.

Nerval answered, in advance, the stupidity of man enclosed within man, incapable of hearing a bleeding heart suffer, incapable of shuddering at the sobs of that pulsing shred of primary flesh nailed to the stars with living-dead Humanity's scratch-marks on his stomach: the poet. Just as he answered the vile, and so foolishly clumsy, attempts to make a Catholic

5. Cf. *Le Mur des Siècles* [The wall of the centuries] by Victor Hugo.
6. *Red metal* is perhaps the metal "which is now only a name," says Plato, "but was then something more, orichalch, which was excavated in various parts of the island (Atlantis), and had then a higher value than any metal except gold" *(Critias).* And I have often dreamt of *blue metal.*

46

of him.[7] As he answered the odious explanations by *sickness, insanity, paranoia, the pathological*, finally, from those doctors who specialize in flies and worms, and who presume to explain dead poets. "I don't know why I use the term 'sickness,' for *never, as far as I am concerned, have I felt better.* At times, I thought my strength and energy were doubled; I seemed to know everything, understand everything. My imagination brought me infinite delight. In recovering what men call reason, do I have to regret the loss of these joys...?"

Earlier, I defined what must be understood by "world." From the primitive chaos of his "psyche," man makes the different planes of the world appear, saying: "that is not myself." As the representation of the negated object expresses none other than the act of negation under specific conditions, so all that exists becomes the symbol of the mind's progress. Now, to stop negating is to sleep. In general, man goes to sleep when he stops distinguishing himself from his sensations; that which forms the primary matter of the dream-world remains un-manifest in him. Some men, having gone to sleep in the physical world (that is, having realized the harmony between the world and themselves, returning to identity after the separation which, by the absurd existence of an external world, created an unbearable imbalance, from which comes movement), awaken in the dream-world and begin a new series of negations ending in the formation of a mode of the universe. And again, in the face of this world, they will seek to identify with it and realize the harmony that must dissolve the individual's discrete existence. Finally, through these clarifications, these successive adjustments, the mind reaches a conscious and definitive identification with That-which-is. According to the Hindus, the Self believes itself identical to itself in three states: waking, dream and deep sleep, the latter corresponding to the supreme Identity. (For the maggot psychology and its ludicrous questions, I will condescend to add: when you say "*my* consciousness," who possesses, and who is possessed? When you

7. When I think of the distance that separates the true meaning of the word "catholic" ("Universal!") from its present meaning, I immediately see the extent of the pretentious infamy on the part of those who group themselves under this label.

say "*I* am unconscious in deep sleep," what does *I* mean? And how, after having slept, could I say that *I* remember *my* consciousness of sleep, if *I*, *me* and *my consciousness* are not identical? That's just it: the whole problem consists in making these terms identical.) Thus, as concisely as possible, Nerval's affirmation has been justified. The same considerations take wholly into account the symbolism that binds the dream to waking life (as the only reality, in both cases, is always an act of consciousness accomplished at the center of an individual case, consequently giving its manifestations a necessary character of universality). They also explain "the effusion of the dream in real life" and allow for the exercise of magic faculties, such as those which allowed Nerval to ward off the Deluge (you have to think of it!) by sacrificing a ring.

But he knew all that! He had resolved to "break down the mystical doors." "Sleep occupies one-third of our lives" (they will never repeat it enough); "after several minutes of numbness a new life begins, free of the conditions of time and space, and certainly the same as that which awaits us after death." That the conditions of the double after death can be partially known even in this life is for me both a metaphysical certainty and a fact of experience.

Aurelia! I speak of *Aurelia* and I have not yet spoken of *Her*, even though she is behind every word I write, shaking my pen. She, in the Pearled Light, while "immense circles were traced in infinity, like the orbs formed in water disturbed by a fallen body," "...smilingly rejected the furtive masks of these various incarnations, and took refuge in the mystical splendors of the Asian sky." She, at the top of the marble stairs, She: "the other night she was sleeping in I don't know which palace, and I could not join her." She, behind the successive masks, behind her many veils, from the obscure curtain of the physical day, passing through increasingly radiant costumes—as one sees those worn by the inhabitants of the *Mysterious City*—to the blinding nudity in which I will be She, the sole object of all love. Beyond the sunless day where the dream-travelers luminously think of her, beyond the sterile lunations of death, She, the identical, immensely stretched out in Deep Sleep without end and in the eternal instant of a point without space, possessed—thus will she be after the bloody road, after the track of deserts stained red by torn knees, after the crossing of bottomless black swamps, after how many human heaps convulsed in tortures! She, the Mysterious Mother, who is the Spirit of the Valley and the Door—you knew it, Ancient Child![8] She, who also in Babylon was called Star: Ishtar, her celestial name, and *Mami* for the adoring man. "Under her feet turned a wheel, and the gods were her procession." It was Aurelia, and it is Isis the eternal Mother, through the centuries—centuries that live gathered in your own spirit, Nerval, as in mine—whose "suffering image dried, cried or languished": for I am the one who, by not knowing her, tortured her. She is Artemis who was suddenly the garden: "She began to grow under a bright ray of light...she seemed to fade into her own greatness." And one terrible day at the end of the world, she "the Virgin is dead... Eternal night begins, and it will be terrible. What will happen when men realize that there is no more sun?" Lost, found again, lost again and by my fault! Seen too soon, when I was—no, when I *am:* the horrible truth comes none too late beneath my sentence—when I am still unable to reach her; when clearly, lucidly, I drag her through torment, I lacerate her with the roughness of the human skeleton, I twist her by forcing her into human form. "*It is too late!.. She is lost!...* I understand: she made a final attempt to save me; I missed the supreme moment when pardon was still possible..."

"...Eternal Isis, sacred mother and wife," sometimes "with the face of ancient Venus, sometimes as well with the features of the Christian Virgin." She, the Moon, Artemis "the Thirteenth"..."it seemed to me that this star was the refuge of all the souls akin to mine, and I saw it populated with plaintive shadows destined one day to be reborn on Earth..."[9] In She who is everything I love, powerful Maya in all forms, I cannot help but torture you and I hear you moaning in my skin, because I want to be you and I impose on you this absurd mold of human

8. Lao-tse, *Tao-te-Ching*, VI.

9. According to the Vedic texts, in the soul's journey after death the moon represents the limit between the region from which one never returns—arrived at by the "path of the gods"—and the region of rebirths. The souls which follow the "path of the spirits" stay there before returning to the material world. Moreover, this symbol is universal (*Diana*, two-faced like *Janus bi-frons, Janua coeli,* etc.).

form in which you suffer...but eternal, identical to What I become, you also escape from every look and at times (oh, Meyrat! you know what I mean), at times the terrible game of your two-sidedness confounds the endless misery of my human tomb, sometimes troubles the sad, blind valley of my human skin, makes me doubt, and a veil of damp silk rips and floats tirelessly over my face, my eyes full of dust. And—at times—this terrible doubt (oh, when will there be radiant certainty without return, without ever coming back to the carcasses of suffering?), this doubt: what I hold there, that luminous face, ah! will I not suddenly realize, *yet again*, that it is only Her ghost—but you understand, it's enough to make you scream in horror: to see no more than the great she-vampire, the Cadaver of all time, wandering, Lilith the frigid.

(1929.)

OPEN LETTER TO ANDRE BRETON
on the relation of Surrealism to the *Grand Jeu*

You address me in particular in your *Second Surrealist Manifesto;* I therefore owe it to myself to answer you personally. But first I must remind you of the following (which the facts should already have taught you):

The *Grand Jeu* is something of an initiatory community: each of its members does whatever he does to maintain and reinforce the group's spiritual unity. Whoever would like to attract one of us from without, with the naive conviction that he is dealing simply with an individual, would only provoke our laughter. What misleads you is that you constantly have the Surrealists in mind, and you evidently think that the *Grand Jeu* is a similar group. But they are worlds apart. Furthermore, you forget a bit too readily that our accomplishments up to this point have been insufficient. We are forced to admit it; otherwise it would be too easy for you to take us to task on a number of accounts, such as never having spoken of Lautréamont.[1]

The question thus becomes: does the *Grand Jeu* (and not one or the other of its members) have good reasons for preferring to keep its distance from Surrealism (and not—a restriction which to you, but not to us!, must seem more obvious than the first—from one or the other of *its* members)?

And even if I had to choose! You recognized in a sentence from one of my texts the identical goal we pursue. Granted. This identical goal implies on the one hand enemies in common and the same obstacles to destroy, and on the other convergent or parallel lines of research. I recognize that men with our aims are rare. Cowardice, stupidity, laxity of mind, the contagiousness of cretinism and bad faith bring increasingly

1. For your information on this point, you can read the manifesto, signed by all the members of the *Grand Jeu,* published in the magazine *Red,* in Prague, to protest the censorship imposed by official Czechoslovakian morality on the *Cantos of Maldoror.*

dangerous hostilities to bear around these men. They are forced to move closer and closer together and to take a united stand. Would I contribute to this union by going toward Surrealism? That step would be, at very least, ridiculous by its ineffectiveness, since while I would be fattening your group, I would be diminishing ours by just as much. But much more, I fear that today Surrealist activity is only confusion, optical illusion and awkwardness, in both its combat efforts and its creative works.

Struggle against the common enemy? Tell me about it! Let's talk about the famous investigation on the possibilities of collaborative action, and about the meeting which followed! On this point, I refer you to the answer that the *Grand Jeu* had sent you at the time. We affirmed our solidarity with you on the principles of revolutionary action. We still affirm it. For, *while you are attacked from all sides on these principles, they are beyond discussion for us.* You seem to be even less assured of this than we, when you feel the need to elaborate, in quite embarrassing and useless arguments, proofs that Marxism is compatible with Surrealism. I will come back later to the blindness this causes you. For the moment, let me weigh our proclaimed agreement with you about an attitude which is, in a nutshell: leftist Hegelianism rallied to the cause of Marxism, and consequently to the principles of the Third International; against those five hours of irritating debate, diverted from its original aims, completely directed—through personal considerations about individuals whom the nature of our group forced us to judge as being ourselves[2] —against the unity of the *Grand Jeu*. On the same scale, I place the account of these discussions in *Variétés* (June 1929), whose exactness none of us will recognize (as it was written without verification by the Surrealists alone, from memories already too far in the past and necessarily biased). That evening, we had come in all good faith. Gilbert-Lecomte, who was perfectly willing to be accused of madness, but not to be criticized for failing to do everything in his power, had brought a detailed and practical plan for collaborative action (founding of a polemical and satirical review with wide circula-

2. Remember that we had left you sole judge of the confidence you granted your friends; it would not be so easy for us to do this today!

52

tion, showcasing each one's subversive qualities—in particular of several Surrealists, whose abilities in this area we value highly; also creation of a magazine of doctrine and research, organization of surveys, etc.) I was forced to see him, alas, tear this plan up in rage when he left! And today, admit that you don't have a hell of a lot to offer us in the way of revolutionary action!

And in the area of positive research, what have you done since the founding of Surrealism? What have you done, surrounded by certain individuals whose presence at your side never ceases to amaze us? Nine-tenths of those who claim or have claimed the title of "Surrealist" have done no more than apply a technique you discovered. As such, they have only managed to create clichés that render it unusable. So that now I should go to you to induge in your little parlor games, in those pathetic and piddling experiments with what you so inappropriately call the "surreal"? For such entertaining discoveries as the "exquisite corpse" and automatic writing (alone or in groups), I should leave the whole technical apparatus that the *Grand Jeu* is working to build, and to which each of us brings his share of resources! We have, in answer to your *amusing science,* the study of all the processes of depersonalization, a telepathy, of clairvoyance, of mediumism; we have the unlimited field (in every conceivable mental direction) of Hindu yoga, the systematic confrontation of the lyrical and dreamlike fact with the teachings of occult tradition (but *to hell* with the *picturesque* in magic), and those of the so-called primitive mind...and we're not finished yet.

On the ideological level, the results you have gotten, seconded by a small number of your friends, do not do much to attract me. Here as well there is not much to be gained by changing sides. The situation, in fact, required you to struggle on all levels and attack every defensive construction of average human thought. Now, the age of Pico della Mirandola is over. It was thus necessary for the mind to take possession, not of a man, but of a group. You yourself recognized this in your call for close collaboration and perfect cohesion. But the Surrealists have never been this group, and this is what condemns them.

This ideological poverty has its repercussions even on you (anyone else would have been subject to them, furthermore). Thus you are led to make completely untenable declarations, for example: "the time of Baudelairean 'correspondences,' which criticism has managed to turn into a detestable commonplace, is over."[3] It is quite painful to notice that you, Breton, are capable of such an amazing lack of understanding, or such ignorance. Must you be reminded of what the system of correspondences, which Baudelaire took directly from Swedenborg, really is? That it has nothing to do with what you seem to think, but is instead a system of mystic thought and the spirit of participation, negating the discursive schemas of successive causality and of a world divided into individual objects?

But I particularly wish to speak of the fate you reserve for Hegel in your *Second Surrealist Manifesto*. You distinguish between *"idealism properly speaking"* and *"absolute idealism"*; between *"simplistic materialism"* and *"dialectical materialism."* This double distinction is absolutely necessary and correct, and I will always make it myself. Your affirmation of absolute idealism is as clear as can be: "...the idea of love tends to create a being,...the idea of Revolution tends to make the day of this Revolution come about, without which these idols would lose all meaning." And in spite of this, you seem to believe in Hegel's failure! Whereas nothing has yet been done toward realizing his main idea: the perfectibility of human reason and its final identification with the *objective mind* which, thinking the world, creates it. There is nothing to change in Dialectics—whether according to Heraclitus, Plato or Hegel—in order for it to live between our eyes, for it to be the beacon of fate lighting the way for revolutions. We must protect this idea. Perhaps the most serious danger threatening it today is this "simplistic materialism" (supposed materialists, formerly supposed idealists, who then got tired and wanted a system of total relaxation; spiritual spinelessness which makes it so easy for them to tell us: "I'm really a revolutionary, and much more orthodox than you, sir..."). But you are far, André Breton, from having done everything necessary against this new enemy. I'm even afraid that you have let this "materialist" state of mind reign much too close to you at times.[4]

3. Preface to the Delbrouck and Defize exhibit, April 1929.
4. Thus I do not reproach you, as others do, with not having sacrificed absolute idealism to a supposed revolutionary materialism. On the contrary, I find that you do not maintain vigorously enough the correlation—scandalous for some—of Hegelian idealism and dialectical materialism. Absolute idealism in particular demands an uncompromising anti-dualist stance and a veritable asceticism of reason toward absolute Reason. Your thesis on *the rose* makes me fear that this concrete spirit, the soul of dialectics, has competely escaped you.

This is one of the most ardent points of our ideological activity: and on this point, I do not have much to hope for from Surrealism, but everything to hope for from the *Grand Jeu*. It is the same in all fields of our doctrine, because each of us brings his own possibilities of expression entirely to the service of a single mind. Thus Rolland de Renéville is working to establish the multiple coordinates of poetic creation (the essay he is publishing in this issue* is a part of this study); Gilbert-Lecomte is working on a *Vision by Epiphysis* in which he constructs the architecture-of-fire of mystic thought and of the spirit of participation. It was with him—and how could I think in terms other than of our common substance?—that I began my research into experimental metaphysics. And the consequences of our rush toward the *real* (which you poorly name, given your understanding of it, the *surreal*) are terrible and *concrete* in a way quite different from your dialectical and pseudo-prophetic exercises. Indeed, I could from my side send you *signs of understanding;* but must they remain without hope of an anwer?

Ideally, therefore, and in conclusion, if I consider your call as being addressed to the *Grand Jeu*, I note that an agreement of principle on a minimal program would be possible between us, even that a certain collaboration would be desirable. But on the one hand, the confusion that I see holding court in Surrealism, the insufficiency of its program; and on the other hand, the fact that the *Grand Jeu*, if it already possesses a relatively precise plan of activity and a complete ideology, has not yet accomplished more than the very first points on its own program: this dual reason would make any collaboration between us, for the moment, premature at best.

From this simple expression of my thoughts on our relations, you yourself see how impossible it is for me to go toward you at the present time. Taking it from a sufficiently elevated and disinterested perspective, I would not even be afraid of saying: come with us, on the same path, to avoid being lost. If such an invitation seems extremely pretentious, it is only with respect to individual judgments, in no way justifiable before the impersonal spirit. Unfortunately, the paths of terrestrial accomplishments are not those of the Spirit. It is all too certain that

Le Grand Jeu no. 3, 1930.

you, André Breton, cannot come to us. But our respective positions in the world, in the crowd of our common enemies, do not allow us to be unaware of each other. Let us then watch each other from now on, and we will see who, between you and us, goes furthest toward the goal that, at times, you have clearly glimpsed. Thus, when you write: "Everything leads us to believe that there exists a certain point in the mind from which life and death, the real and the imaginary, past and future, the communicable and the incommunicable, top and bottom, stop being perceived as contradictory," it is indeed about the point toward which we strive; about the point at which, finally, we will meet you, and on the road to which we leave all possible hopes murdered behind us. And, rejecting those who, as you say, "continue to care somewhat about the position they will occupy *in the world*," we are certainly the most lucid of those seekers who have devoted their lives to that nameless identity; the most pitiless for those who, by force, cunning or sophism, oppose our march. Whereas you, toward whom we were once able to turn our gaze the way we would look toward a guide whose function was to lead men both far from and close to themselves—you run a strong risk of remaining paralyzed, caught in the traps that you have set for yourself, and in those that your extraordinary blindness has allowed your enemies, disguised or not, to set for you. Beware, André Breton, of eventually figuring in study guides to literary history; whereas if we aspired to an honor, it would be that of being inscribed for posterity in the history of cataclysms.

…But after all these reservations, which bear only on the possibility and timeliness of imminent material collaboration, be aware, André Breton, that if, in the absence of an external Event imperious enough to require our immediate reconciliation, we are far from being ready to work together, be aware that we continue nonetheless to look upon you as one of the few men who go, without betrayal, on the only path we allow ourselves to follow. For once—and we insist on declaring this for all to hear—you have before you men who, all the while keeping their distance from you, often severely criticizing you, are still not about to vomit their basest insults on you. If we cannot undertake anything definite with you for the moment, if we have reproaches to level at you, it will in no case be your moral person that we attack: to us, that always appears, from near or from afar, as intact as ever. And more than temporal disagreements or shifts in mood are enough to destroy the esteem inspired in us by a man possessed by the same Search to which we, like him, have sacrificed everything.

(1930.)

SURREALISM AND THE *GRAND JEU*

In abstracto, the Surrealists occupy an historical position which is also that of the *Grand Jeu.* Having attained knowledge of the dialectical necessity of revolution, they note that their activity is the intellectual aspect of revolutionary force, whose physical aspect is the proletariat. Their aim is this: to serve the proletarian Revolution by describing "the real workings of the mind." Their role would thus be to instill a knowledge of the mind, regulated by dialectics, capable of annihilating those illusory psychologies which, taking advantage of the absence of revolutionary doctrine in this domain, continue to cover our humanity with its mould.

Correlative problem: to find the means of making oneself understood, not by the snobbish and dilettantish bourgeois public, but by true revolutionary thinkers.

In reality, this sought-after psychological doctrine does not yet exist. Surrealism's techniques might constitute an excellent means of investigation into certain domains, if they are taken as simple techniques. Unfortunately, automatic writing, dream inducement, etc., all too quickly become for the Surrealists *"means of thinking," thinking mechanisms,* in other words processes to sleep by, so as not to have to think. The original vice of Surrealism, which is *the* universal human vice, is precisely that search for a Thinking Machine. There are no *means* of thinking: I think, immediately, or I sleep.

The absence of this single criterion, consciousness, throws a certain confusion into Surrealist research. Sometimes aware of what "dialectical materialism" is in its essence (knowledge of the world as being that of a *matter* whose mode of existence is *movement),* all too often they fall back into old materialism ("primacy of matter over thought"), which is never more than a lame dualism (as old idealism, which excludes matter, is a lame dualism). When their thought stumbles, it is always to *this* materialism that they cling: another means, a system foreign to them and artificial, a trick to avoid thinking.

Our role, which should be theirs, is essentially:

to describe matter, which is movement;
the various modes of movement: rhythms;
the various aspects of the concrete: physical, biological, psychological, as modes of movement subject to certain determined rhythms;
dialectics as rhythmic activity in all domains, etc.

No realm of human knowledge can escape this investigation; but this demands a perpetual effort of thinking—of thinking dialectically, not according to a dialectical logic. For too many "materialists," what in fact exists, despite what they say, is not matter, but the idea of matter. In this case, they will remain disguised idealists, as long as they have not grasped the relation which exists between the movement "idea of pebble" and the movement "pebble."

In the same way, we judge quite insufficient the so-called "materialist" critiques of religion which, basically, are almost always no more than merely sensualist. We will talk about this elsewhere.

Finally, the lack of unity and sureness in the pursuit of the real (again from a lack of awareness) allowed almost every reader of the last few issues of *Le Surréalisme au Service de la Révolution* [Surrealism in the service of revolution] to make all-too-easy jokes about the use of leisure time by workers in the society of the future, etc. None of the Surrealists, taken separately, is responsible for this; but the juxtaposition of a study by T. Tzara and a "daydream" by S. Dali unfailingly suggests some rather regrettable images, which we do not wish to help peddle here.

(1930-31.)

59

LAUTREAMONT AND THE CRITICS

Any poetical work, if it is worthy of this name, is such by virtue of a dialectical knot, a moment in the mind that it embodies and signifies. Just as much as the fruit of a past evolution, it heralds the future development of the seeds it carries. And men, so hasty to judge, are split into two camps once they have done so. Those of the first camp recognize in the work the very movement of this spirit and of the world; and, seeing themselves prophesied, they admire. The others, if they are not totally blind, tremble more or less consciously before the all-too-obvious image of a destiny that their mental laziness, cowardice and egotism cannot accept; they reject and attack it. The critic's role is to make the work known as a dialectical crossroads to a public of the first kind, and to defend it against the second.

On these grounds, Lautréamont's work especially deserves the name of poetry; for it contains *in itself*—which is rare—both the absolutely stated thesis and the antithesis. Now, no one had analyzed what dialectical steps unavoidably followed each other in the *Cantos of Maldoror* and the *Poesies*; no one had unraveled the rigorous ribbon which dramatically thinks up and calculates itself; no one had been the critic of Lautréamont before Léon Pierre-Quint published *Count Lautréamont and God.*[1] We could have, and this is saying a lot, expected as much from him. At least those readers who have long recognized in Léon

1. *Le Comte de Lautréamont et Dieu* by Léon Pierre-Quint (Editions des Cahiers du Sud, 1928). Jacques Spitz, in the August issue of the *Nouvelle Revue Française,* has already expressed his opinion of this book. Reading his note has convinced me that from now on even a pleasantly disdainful silence on the part of those who must and who can defend Lautréamont would be veritable treason. It is necessary today to recall what the attitudes were, and what the function of criticism must be, with respect to Isidore Ducasse.

Pierre-Quint one of the few critics who are honest with themselves, with the works criticized, and with the public; a critic having as principle (his work on Proust in particular bears witness) to seek to render an author's thought living, true and effective, by accounting for everything that is concrete in the man and the work as if they were his own actions; a critic who never closes his eyes to the chain of "Why's?" that endlessly unwinds in the alert mind—those readers could have expected as much. If I wished to describe the intimate process of Lautréamont's poetry schematically, I would essentially find myself summarizing Léon Pierre-Quint's book, a coincidence which owes nothing to chance.

Maldoror stands as the complete man in revolt, in a struggle with neither quarter nor mercy against a God who has always been the supreme object of human revolt. Against the demiurge he is great like Cain, like Prometheus, like a given Gnostic philosophy or one of William Blake's creatures. Maldoror wants the absolute immediately. He obtains it by erecting as absolute his own consciousness, the lucid consciousness of a man whose powers of understanding frighteningly exceed his powers of possession—in such a way that by standing against God, fleeing every kind of sleep, he raises human intelligence and its purest manifestation, mathematics, to a very elevated position. But this human absolute is universal; thus Maldoror empathizes (Léon Pierre-Quint is the first to underline this) with every conscious man in revolt, with every man who has not yet been corrupted by God's gift of civilization, with the child and the adolescent. These beings he loves; he wants to lead their implacable struggle against the family, school, religion, justice, against all those bonds, and against that which unites them: the awareness of good and evil.

But the world does not change one iota just because one renounces it. In order to change it, one must begin by submitting to it. One must kill oneself—and even then wouldn't one have to die immediately, through a simple act of will?—or renounce absolute revolt, which is a pure abstract moment developing contradictions in itself as soon as it tries to pass into existence. This is not abdication: the mind becomes aware of this contradiction and institutes a new state of revolt. It places revolt inside itself as the only reality, the material world becoming simple appearance. This is the *idealistic moment* of revolt. Its primary sign is *humor,* "sense of the theatrical — and joyless — pointlessness of everything," according to Jacques Vaché.[2] *Humor,* an idealistic moment in human activity, and the profound *love* engendered in Maldoror by the sense of his damned solidarity with the free man against God, gives birth to *sadism,* sexual humor. Poetically, the mind's movement in the self becomes all-powerful *inspiration,* creator or revealer of a marvelous world, that of dreams, where everything is possible, where revolt finds satisfaction.

Thus the "great themes" of the *Cantos of Maldoror,* as Léon Pierre-Quint enumerates them, arise from the contradictions cropping up in the very heart of the attitude of complete revolt, in particular humor, sadism, inspiration, the marvelous. The mere expression of their dialectical resolution in a poem would have been enough to insure this poem's greatness.

Lautréamont did not stop there. He seemingly makes an about-face to criticize this idealistic stage of revolt, or at least its expression, and thus the *Poésies: "reductio ad absurdam"* of the vanity of affirming or negating, "infernal machine" placed in the apparatus of thought, to use Mr. Jean Paulhan's expressions,[3] as quoted by Léon Pierre-Quint. A. Rolland de Renéville, comparing this opinion with that of the Surrealists (who understood the *Poésies* as a definitive rejection of any artistic manifestation) and following a personal observation, said exactly what must be said: "These three hypotheses, far from being contradictory, complement each other; the result is that the opposites give rise to one another by an act of inversion, that they are interchangeable, and that their confrontation brings about the absence of all activity in favor of an incommunicable light."[4]

Now, in this incommunicable light subsists the entire dynamic content of primary revolt, and Lautréamont's work, closing in on itself, becomes the seed of future development. Having reached silent unity, the mind will notice that it is the same for the progression of phenomena as for that of thought: it will see each tangible aspect of the universe devour itself, following an unchangeable dialectic. By subscribing to this perpetual

2. Jacques Vaché, *Lettres de guerre* [War letters].
3. Jean Paulhan, *Jacob Cow le pirate ou Si les mots sont des signes* [Jacob Cow the pirate, or If words are signs].
4. A. Rolland de Renéville, in *Cahiers du Sud,* April 1930.

movement, the man in revolt will finally be able to *realize* his revolt by becoming a revolutionary. He sees this passage, which is accomplished in his individual development from child to adult, etched in political, social and even literary history. Popular uprisings are organized into class struggle. The Surrealists, having closed the same circle as Lautréamont—from complete revolt to universal humor—are trying to get out of it through Marxism. It is enough that the seed bequeathed by our ancestor Isidore Ducasse germinates in a few minds, in order that, step by step, consciousnesses are enflamed and the old suppressed revolts flare out into Revolution.

There's the "infernal machine," all right! But phenomenal appearance, particularly social appearance, threatened by this dialectic, resists and defends itself. One by one, all the enemies that Society always brings to bear against true poets spring up around Lautréamont. First there are the vulgar attacks. They try, for example, to show that Lautréamont was a mythical figure, and that the *Cantos of Maldoror* are a literary joke; several critics wished to see them as a hoax perpetrated by Rémy de Gourmont.[5] "I have been assured," says Mr. Marcel Arland,[6] "and I tend to believe it, that Lautréamont was one of Victor Cousin's pseudonyms." Or else, they call these *Cantos* the work of a madman; you have to see, in the issue of *Disque Vert* devoted to the *Lautréamont Case* in 1925, how this opinion of Léon Bloy's and Rémy de Gourmont's is taken up by Laurent Tailhade, Albert Thibaudet, Maeterlinck ("…more or less voluntary dementia and fermentation of the pale treponema," says the latter). For Henri de Régnier,[7] the *Cantos of Maldoror* are a "strange mass of wild fantasies," a "farrago of raving insanities." Finally, they try to present Lautréamont's work as simple literary ramblings, to classify it among "…those works whose strictly external audacity is easily imitated," as Mr. René Lalou does.[8]

Here, we are reaching the most serious—because the most insidious—attacks. They try to weaken the true power of the *Cantos of Maldoror* by coming to their defense, but on a purely literary level. Lautréamont becomes a talented poet, an admirable stylist, a master of lyricism, of the epic, of the detective

5. Cf. *Le Quotidien*, March 11, 1930.
6. "Le Cas Lautréamont," in *Le Disque Vert*, 1925.
7. *Le Figaro*, May 6, 1930.
8. *Les Nouvelles Littéraires*, April 26, 1930.

novel, of irony, a great and quite harmless writer. They go further: they make him a sacred figure, which they create arbitrarily if necessary—Philippe Soupault did not do Lautréamont any favors by erecting his "Ducasse."[9] They incite snobbery around him; they affect intimacy with the poet to keep others from touching him. Thus Jean Cocteau, taking fright at seeing the Surrealists try to impose before the world the shadows of Rimbaud and Lautréamont as they are, wrote in this same *Disque Vert:* "The firm of Isidore-Arthur and Co., only Max [Jacob], Radiguet and I sniffed the thing out. . . but I am proud to be alone in such company." Thus, whether one prostitutes the poet or hides him, it is toward the same end: to strip him of his explosive power.

There are two possible paths for bringing the true Lautréamont to light and defending him against his enemies. One is negative, the other affirmative. The negative path is particularly that of André Breton. Lautréamont is *not* a talented poet, admirable stylist, master of lyricism, the epic, the detective novel or irony; is *not* the close friend of Mr. So-and-so; is *not* a colorful eccentric. We must save Lautréamont from the attempts at corruption and castration exerted on him. We must prevent him from being admired in the name of a value which, whatever it might be, he would have renounced in advance. And we must also impose him as such, for it is not a matter of hermeticism for André Breton: "I consider," said André Gide (and rightly so), "the crowning glory of the group formed by Breton, Aragon and Soupault to be having recognized and proclaimed the literary and ultra-literary importance of the admirable Lautréamont."

As a dialectician, André Breton, having negated in Lautréamont all the attributes under which others sought to stifle him, could only rejoice at seeing Léon Pierre-Quint undertake his defense by the only possible affirmative path, one supported by a sure dialectic. This meeting, by a single demonstration, of two opposing paths is striking enough for me to emphasize it. It is remarkable that Breton "very strongly approves"; and he says so, he claims, because Pierre-Quint's idea to *"speak* of Lautréamont...was against all hope."[10]

Because Pierre-Quint has grasped the central point of

9. Preface to the complete edition of Lautréamont's works (Au Sans Pareil, 1927).

Lautréamont's poetry and revolt, because he has freed Lautréamont from all the false costumes in which many sought to conceal him, he has been able to *talk* of him positively, in the only way one could speak of him: by guaranteeing the work the one position capable of restoring all its effectiveness. "He has left him his terrible greatness, his shattering mixture of human weakness and destructive force, his marvelous lucidity with its dazzling detours."[11] He has done it first by reuniting all the facets of the poet of Maldoror in the same dialectical movement; whence the accent of his book: clear, not with the clarity of a popularization, but with the rigorous clarity of mathematics. For, rather than bring judgment, he endeavors to illuminate the detours of a living thought, henceforth preventing any clouded or fallacious judgment from seducing the mind toward shadow. And this thought is also living, victorious over the undertakers of the spirit, through what Pierre-Quint lends it of his life and ours. The better to shoot down all hope of our seeing in Lautréamont's work only literature or outrageousness of expression without concrete consequences, he gives himself bodily, with memories of childhood and holidays, to the Count's thought. We can almost touch these horrible sufferings of escaped convicts, we can experience them. If Léon Pierre-Quint compares them to Maldoror's torments, are these torments then just as real? Is *that* the danger of taking the path of revolt? Yes, we are finally forced to know what a work such as Isidore Ducasse's involves us in; forced to know that if the "infernal machine" explodes, it will be no laughing matter. The petty literary thrills are finished at last. At last, it indeed concerns our human carcasses present here. At last, we see clearly.

(1930.)

10. It is unfortunately difficult for me to quote these remarks at greater length here, as Breton has only expressed himself on this subject in private correspondence and conversation. But I would state my thoughts exactly by repeating verbatim certain terms of a letter from Breton, in which he says to Léon Pierre-Quint about his book: "This saves us from literally half a century to come of idiocy, of trying *not* to understand him by the usual means... I completely admire the conduct of your thought in this book, and the increasing clarity which lays hold of the things you look at. And the apparent absence of passion which makes you – like me – definitively confuse things passionate with things reasonable."

11. G. Ribemont-Dessaignes, in *Europe*, September 15, 1930.

ASPHYXIATION AND ABSURD EVIDENCE*

Agreement among men cannot be founded on a general theory unless this theory allows for experimental verification. This is the problem with metaphysics, if it remains merely an effort to logically coordinate abstract notions without discussing their origins. All general knowledge is only potential, and the logical coordination of its elements allows for no more than the possibility of knowing. But a metaphysics conceived as the anticipated knowledge of a possible progress of consciousness can call upon the very experience of consciousness. It then becomes the science of what we can immediately grasp, and by means of which all our other knowledge is grasped; thus the science of science: supreme science.

I will here summarize everything that one experiment in particular, which I will then describe, allows me to think of as true.[1]

I. Something absurd can be intuited.

II. A mind long accustomed to thinking in certain ways and under certain conditions, if placed in other conditions requiring another means of thinking, no longer thinks — in other words, it sleeps.

III. Despite the very large community that exists between the ways of thinking of different human individuals (in particular, those belonging to the same civilization), we can find in some of them several minor differences.

*This essay was originally scheduled for Le Grand Jeu no. 4, under the title: "The First Revelation of Experimental Metaphysics: the Unrelatable Experience."

1. This example, if it is among the most striking, is not perfectly pure. It concerns an experience which is, in fact, shattering for whoever can stand it, but which is not within everyone's reach. It is only when we expose the complete method of this experimental ontology that we will be able to suggest simpler, more direct experiments, that all minds can perform.

IV. It happens, therefore, that under certain specific and identical conditions, one man will sleep without dreaming and another will think: the first, because he cannot think outside of his customary forms and conditions, the second because he is freed from them.

V. If a mind can only grasp itself in such forms and conditions of thought, it is because it does not distinguish these forms and conditions from thought itself.

VI. For the majority of Westerners of our century in particular, the logical forms of thought are confused with the act of thinking itself. Thus, if one of them finds himself placed in conditions such that, were he freed from these forms, the intuition of something absurd is given to him, he sleeps.

VII. Now, such conditions happen to correspond to easily attainable psychological states, such as certain beginnings of asphyxiation, of narcosis, certain feverish states.

VIII. In similar circumstances, most men find themselves in a state of sleep or delirium without memory. But some, freer of the customary forms of thought, see these circumstances as an occasion to think in complete lucidity, according to ways insurmountable to vulgar logic (but not to all logic; for example, the identity of opposites, foundation of dialectical logic, can in such cases become an *intuitive* evidence).

IX. When these circumstances are attained accidentally or artificially, the way of thinking occasioned by them establishes itself only temporarily: the mind is already able to stand such thoughts, not yet to bring them about at will, and this feeling of impotence is a suffering which virtually defies expression. But this experience (anticipated, so to speak, by a kind of fraud) of new conditions of thought allows one to conceive of a voluntary progress of the mind distinguishing and freeing itself by degrees from the forms in which it successively perceives itself.

Such were (in 1924) my first experiences of this kind of phenomenon:

One day, I deeply inhaled vapors of carbon tetrachloride "to see what would happen"; the results surpassed anything I could have imagined. I repeated the experiment several times. Each time, in a completely singular fashion, this is what happened:

After a whole series of phenomena quite familiar to those who have undergone general anaesthesia (sound of a combustion engine, swarm of bright spots, etc.), the phosphenes suddenly became so intense that, even with my eyes open, they formed a veil before me which prevented me from seeing anything else. At the same time they arranged themselves in a mosaic of circles and triangles—black, red and white—inscribing and circumscribing each other and moving according to a rigorous but geometrically absurd law. This movement which, as far as I could tell, went according to an immobile spiral, followed a rhythm: that of the increasingly acute and rapid sound of an engine. I then noticed that this rhythm was also that of the pounding of blood in my temples and, under pain of irreparable loss, and always to the same accelerated rhythm, I had to repeat an unpronounceable word (approximately: "temgwef temgwef drrr..."). At a certain moment, the rhythm became so rapid that I could no longer follow it, and suddenly I *recognized* the truth I had always known, I awoke to this truth. With an evidence, a clarity which I cannot begin to relate—so much is this character of certainty, of absolute necessity, unknown to normal human thought—I understood the meaning of this visual and sonorous movement, appalling, maddening both in its simplicity and in its obviousness. The last word of everything, the explanation, spoken by the voice of an absolutely cruel irony, of the existence of my mind, was contained in a kind of supra-logical and terribly simple reasoning, impossible to translate. I have never accepted, and could never accept, the Christian belief in eternal loss and damnation. And yet, at that moment—which I can, if I wish, recapture in several minutes—I was certain, with a simple and glaring certainty, that I, myself, the only being, was irrevocably *lost* (and the word "loss" is still only a remote approximation): *that I was nothing more than a very simple vicious circle.* And at the same time I told myself (for if my life in its "normal" state now appeared a flimsy illusion, I had at no time lost contact with it): "In a few hours all this will be over, but for now I know the truth, and later I will make the mistake of forgetting this eternal evidence."

Despite that evidence, I persist in thinking this (otherwise, I would have no choice but to go crazy or kill myself, for next to such a certainty, life, death, reason and insanity are really *of no consequence*): this feeling of irreparableness is the highest degree of certainty that the human mind as such can attain; it is not absolute certainty. In this experience, I am placed under such conditions of thought that the mind of the human individual that I am becomes aware of its inherent contradiction which, resolving itself, leads it necessarily to its downfall. But, as these conditions were established accidentally, and not through a conscious effort of liberation, this temporary dissolution of the mind seems to me an absurd *fatality*, instead of being thought of clearly as a *necessity*. I am aware of my irrevocable downfall as a man, without already being able to think of myself outside of human forms. This condition of endless despair and suffering would be the human mind's if it were eternal; and if I have encountered it, it is because I wished to consider myself at the limits of eternity, all the while remaining a man. And I am led to think that by a willful effort of the mind I could one day establish the same conditions of awareness. But the despair of human consciousness will then be erased by the brighter clarity of an apprehension of oneself in a higher, freer mode.

I have observed the same phenomenon while inhaling the vapors of ether. Now, there are a number of ether addicts who are completely unaware of this revelation, probably because, having reached the critical point, they can no longer think, and fall asleep. Otherwise, this despair, this superhuman suffering, would soon cure them of their addiction: it is impossible for a man to withstand *that* on a daily basis.[2]

Finally, once having had to undergo general anaesthesia by nitrous oxide (so-called "laughing gas," which I will readily understand if I think of a certain horrible LAUGH, provoked by the *sight of absurdity*), I immediately *recognized* the same certainty, the same anguish (I believe that it would be the same with chloroform or any other general anaesthetic). And while under

2. Furthermore, I believe it is the same for every addict. If he remained conscious when his body entered the realm of sleep, he would, I am convinced, find himself bound in a circle of irrevocable distress similar to the one I tried to translate into words. And the euphoria he had sought—as well as its counterpart, the torture of need—would be *nothing* compared to this superhuman ordeal. This is why the possibility, for a man, of an experience such as the one I described is completely contradictory to the taste for mind-altering drugs.

the mask, I thought to myself that almost any other man, in my place, at that instant, would already have been asleep. And I probably *did* fall asleep for a moment—perhaps a second—later than another patient would have done.

I said "almost any other man." Indeed, for a long time, I knew only Gilbert-Lecomte who, with no possible doubt, understood exactly WHAT it was about, from having experienced it himself. Today I suspect that several other rare individuals around me know THAT. But human language is so insufficent in this domain that I cannot be totally sure.

Despite the impossibility—essential to the fact I am relating as well as I can—of expressing it adequately, whoever has had the experience will, on reading my attempt at narration, immediately recognize (and this is absolutely certain) that I am speaking of *the same thing.* And I see no way for him not to admit having reached the same metaphysical conclusions as those described above, resulting from my own reflection on this experience.

I stress that for an intuition of the absurd to acquire its full value as metaphysical experience, it is not necessary for you to recreate the specific and rather exceptional experiment that I have related. But the existence of each and every thing in the world, the presence of consciousnesses distinct from yours, your own existence, finally, as an individual and finite being—all of that must, if you really awaken, appear intolerably absurd to you. You must begin by considering absolutely unresolvable the double question: why does anything exist? why does this thing exist? All that you are given must become, before anything else, a *subject of Scandal.*

(1930-31.)

THE ROLE OF MOVEMENT IN THE COMPLETE EDUCATION OF MAN

Sometimes one of life's accidents – misfortune, a deeply moving encounter – rattles the relatively factitious and solid edifice that a human being has built up for the comfort of his existence. Shaken to what he believes to be his roots, he is burned for an instant by the fire of a question, a doubt: who am I? why am I living? where am I going? At this moment of reality, he thinks. But such moments are almost always exceptional and accidental, particularly for the specialized men – conditioned by social attitudes, withdrawn into vicious circles in the shadows of their consciousness – that our modern civilization produces in abundance. But the edifice's semblance of balance is rarely compromised in a serious way. For the question "who am I," civil status, first names, last names, positions, professions, titles, ranks, social circles, mirrors, ambitions, vanities and laziness are there to give the pretense of an answer. If the person is of a slightly speculative nature, his little internal philosophy also keeps answers to these rattling questions – brilliant, consoling or approximative answers – in reserve. And man, that phantom vessel, sets off again under his illusory rigging on the waves of this world where, at times, a real vessel leaves its wake.

Moreover, how would he have resolved these questions? Even looking at them straight on – as in Jacob's time men confronted blazing angels on mountaintops and struggled with them, burning their limbs – what could he do? Where to begin? It is difficult to start questioning everything if one has not seen or at very least heard of an open way, no matter how hard or narrow it might be, in the search for a real answer. But in the miraculous logic of life, it seems that every true search will find the external help, the road-signs it needs: not a vehicle which would transport man effortlessly, in which he could rest and let himself be driven, but a precise finger which always shows the most direct, and the harshest, path, in an area where each one, to go forward, can only count on his own effort

What to do, where to begin for those whom doubt has shaken, for those who have not lost the childhood desire to seek themselves, to experience themselves, to build themselves? And what to do to spare the child experiences which are often long and painful, to guide him along a path of normal human development (I do not mean conforming to external and arbitrary rules, but following the real and complete evolution of the consciousness invested in a human individual)? There is no lack of educators or supposed instructors who believe or make believe that they have found the key, the ideal system. In reality, these systems almost always center on an idea or observation that is true, but partial. For one, the perfect education will be the fully natural, animal development of the human beast; for another, the cultivation of spontaneity and sensitivity above all; for a third, the methodic exercise of intellectual faculties. Almost always, they will place the accent on a particular discipline dear to them: physical culture, sports, camping, painting, music, philosophy or natural history. Almost always, they are men with hearts full of good intentions; and some of them are eminently dangerous because they uniformly impose their good intentions, their limited concepts, their manias or even their tics on the students confided to them, without realizing that a given educational method, excellent for one, will make the other a mental cripple.

If I have spoken of a miraculous logic of life, it is because at a time when the need for it in all of us is so great, I have seen in action a method of education, in the exact meaning of the word, capable of indicating to each one, child or adult, the truest direction in which to search for himself. Not only of indicating, but, by an incessant call to the consciousness and presence of the total individual, by exercises, conditions and experiments appropriate to each one, of inciting each one to walk, blossom and ripen in this path on which each one goes alone, in the solitude of a single presence which is nonetheless the place where we can all communicate.

The fact is that there exists a teaching founded on this knowledge, which can address every human being because it addresses every aspect of the human being. Not by compiling various methods and teachings, as do most current "educational" institutions, which believe they can develop the whole being by adding together one hour of mathematics, one hour of drawing and one hour of gymnastics, thus cutting the individual into little slices, whose center of centers, dispersed, is lost; but rather, by first asking each one to be present as he is, at that very moment, with all he possesses in organs, faculties and acquisitions, from head to foot via the heart. And the only form of existence common to the diverse aspects of the individual being, which will thus be the means, the grounds of this teaching, is movement. If someone says, the same as of the moving body, that one is "emotionally moved," that "thought races," these metaphors are not simply rhetorical figures. All of this is movement. And all movement is subject to a speed (a tempo), a cadence and a rhythm. The science—not only theoretical, but lived—of speeds, cadences and rhythms will thus be a choice means for a genuine education. This practical science has several aspects. Two of the main ones are or were known under the names of dance and music: arts, not as the digestive, emotional or intellectual gratifications we usually know, but as a superior know-how, a knowing-how-to-make-oneself, in the sense that Music for the Greeks enveloped all culture; in the sense that Poetry is creation, edification of the self.

But still I fear, by this theoretical display, that I am veering away from the central fact. I would like to make you attend one of these "lessons," or rather one of these life-concentrates. But no, it would not be enough for you to see and hear; even repeated over and over, the sight would always have something new, you would feel that work was being done, that something was on the move, but it would still be an external sight.

A whole other landscape, which opens in the self, appears to him who takes part (if only once) in these "lessons." First, there is an internal chaos, a profound confusion; everything is put back into question. They ask you to make very simple gestures: your body no longer obeys as soon as you step slightly away from your old habits. They ask you to express a very simple feeling and you remain expressionless, or with inappropriate expressions, as soon as you are stripped of your learned attitudes and conventional masks. They ask you to make a very simple effort of memory, reflection, calculation, and your intelligence works only with great pain as soon as your associative mechanisms, your set expressions and your clichés have fallen in cold ashes on your brains and tongues. This experience, with which life is stingy, is offered you at every moment. Every minute, you see a bit more clearly all that is mechanism, death, sleep, cowardice, pose, vanity, chatter, in the various formations of your being. But you will not be crushed by despair, for you will see an open path, a way to settle into the flickering, poor and naked glimmer which, with eclipses, glows in you. You will see a way to revive this little flame, to feed it, to make it grow and last and rush onto the free path that it must light. Then you will understand that when the pupil who had such difficulty with the simple act of walking suddenly lights up with joy and ease, it is because this joy is the sign that, finally, he has really performed the action of walking at a given pace — not made the physical pretense of walking, but has consciously walked at this pace, harmonizing his torso with his legs, his head with his heart, and his heart with his feet. You will know what this joy can mean from real contact with yourself, when it rises up in you, when not only a simple pace but an entire rhythm comes to life in your body. In your heart, you will discover treasures and manure heaps. You will see your brain working, your blatant theories, the mouldy libraries that encumber the room upstairs. And perhaps, at that moment, an eye will open inside your skull, and will shoo out flocks of chattering parrots. You will see what those who stood stock-still saw: what jungles, what aviaries, what menageries full of cries, murmurs, growls, what a realm of which you are king, and what disorder the country has fallen into because the prince was sleeping or dreaming of distant nations. And time will seem very short indeed. There is so much clearing out to do, so much order to establish and so many orders to give.

Sometimes, the voice that externally directs you will point out that a given muscle in your body is too tense, or not tense enough; that a given nerve is uselessly irritated; or that your mind is wandering into other lands. You will know that this was true, you will pull yourself together. Little by little a profound operation, whose only visible sign is a joy, a relaxation, a sudden ease in your entire body, will be accomplished in you. And little by little, you will begin to seek, in the acts of your life, that consciousness of being here. More clarity, more justice and judiciousness will develop in your gestures, your works, your rest and your daily relations. Or sometimes that voice will speak a little longer, and its words will fall on you as onto well-ploughed earth, whereas for another they would have inspired only sterile curiosity.

Since we must give everything a name, when someone asks Mme. de S. what her "courses" consist of, she generally answers that they consist of *movement*. The word has the double advantage of being exact, provided one takes it in its complete sense, and of being safe from label-stickers of every category, from every something-ism. By appropriate movements of all kinds (including the active and conscious immobility which is an absolute mode of movement), by suggesting speeds, paces and rhythms to an individual's diverse activities, such a method guides him along paths at whose bends he inevitably meets an often unexpected side of himself. Man can thus, step by step, manage to weigh what he is worth, what he is capable of; to command with appropriate economy, for the best possible return, the resources, reserves, transformations and uses of his energy—in all the aspects in which it manifests itself; to move body, feelings and thought in mutual balance toward his goal; to know what he wants to do and to do it, to love doing it, to want what he does.

(1934.)

THE POWERS OF THE WORD

The *"Phrères Simplistes."* Left to right: René Daumal, Roger Gilbert-Lecomte, Robert Meyrat, and Roger Vailland

The four Simplists in Reims, 1929. Clockwise: Vailland, Gilbert-Lecomte, Meyrat, Daumal. They were in their final year of lycèe

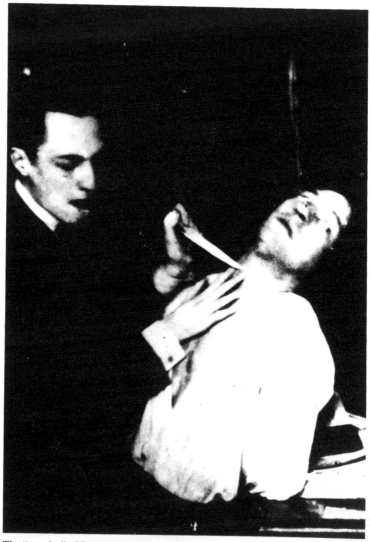

The "murder" of Daumal by Gilbert-Lecomte,
in the manner of horror films

Daumal in the 1930s

Daumal in Indian dress, assuming the padmasana (lotus) yoga position, 1937. Padmasana, the ordinary position for worship, is believed to cure any kind of sickness

Rene Daumal as photographed by Luc Dietrich on May 19, 1944, three days before his death.

THE LIMITS OF PHILOSOPHICAL LANGUAGE AND TRADITIONAL KNOWLEDGE

1. Specific aims of General Philosophy.

The very name "philosophy" gives us to understand that it is not an end in itself. Socrates, with his badgering good sense, said that the philosopher cannot possess wisdom, since "philosopher" means he who loves or seeks wisdom.

Now that philosophy has been divided into branches, the various disciplines which compose it have retained this characteristic of not being ends in themselves. Logic only becomes fruitful by running up against the illogicalities – or at least the irreducibles – of real existence. The identity principle, in itself a pure tautology, only becomes real thought when confronted with a contradictory or changing existence. Philosophy of science teaches us nothing by itself, and by itself gives us no power to act; its outcome is in the scientist's laboratory or the engineer's building-site. Aesthetics in itself contains nothing beautiful; its end and its realization are in artistic creation and judgment. Moral philosophy as such has no moral content; it only finds this in the activity of a living man.

Thus, it is clear for each of these three examples – scientific, aesthetic and moral philosophy – that we are in the presence of special languages aiming toward other-than-verbal ends; of three great forms of philosophical Discourse which, in order to be accomplished, require three kinds of human action – actions no longer of simple discourse, but in which body and thought are simultaneously enlisted.

We are left with what nobody these days still dares call metaphysics, which, for lack of a better rubric, we place under the heading of General Philosphy. If we look at the ensemble of Philosophy today from the outside, in its objective forms – that is, first and foremost in its scholarly institutions – we see that the analogy of the three preceding branches does not apply to General Philosophy.

The Philosophy of Science, in the final account, becomes part of scientific and technical education; Aesthetics part of artistic and literary education; and Moral Philosophy part of moral or civic education. But wherever General Philosophy tries to go, it doesn't fit. It seems to remain in its discursive realm and attain its goal only in books and systems. Then, would this General Philosophy, which claims to encompass all other branches of philosophy, be the only one to fall prisoner to words, while the other forms of speculation are freed from them through their realization in human actions? This seems to be readily admitted. In this case, one either condemns it under the name "metaphysics" as being no more than vain speculation, or one admits that the Discourses it engenders have value in themselves, independent of any non-verbal accomplishment. In both cases, we have forgotten to define the aim of this "General Philosophy," which is indeed the "Philosophy" which Socrates spoke about, and which for him was inquiry and means, not outcome and end.

Logic tends toward knowledge, Aesthetics toward feeling, Morals toward action. If we wish to give General Philosophy a meaning which will prevent it from being subsumed under these other branches, but which will embrace these three specific aims without being simply their juxtaposition, we can only give it *Being* as an end. Not the abstract Being of the logician, for this would be to fall back into logic. But real Being, which simultaneously thinks, feels and acts; the Being which brings about, or rather which *should* bring about, the unity of these three functions of human life. I say: "which should bring about the unity," for this unity is not; this Being does not exist, so long as we need to philosophize. If it existed, we would not have to look for it.[1] Now, one can find worthwhile, educated and virtuous artists who nonetheless feel the need to philosophize. Even if the best results of the cultivation of intelligence, sensitivity and action are united in a single individual, one will not necessarily have a unified man. These functions will rarely be directed toward a single goal, with none suppressing the others and all three subject to a single, real center to the single coachman of this triple harness.

1. But we would not, on the other hand, look for it if we didn't have something like the memory of having found and then lost it.

No verbal discipline can awaken this center of Being. But if it happens to shine, or if in the individual's core it simply begins to stir the tenacious itch of the will to be, it lights all languages with a new flame.

In this respect, it is worthwhile to observe the blooming of philosophical understanding in a high-school Philosophy class. Almost always, the pupil to whom one assigns the writing of a first philosophical essay will treat it as he would treat his "compositions" or his geometry problems. He will not see any vital importance in it; he will see the Philosophy course as a rather disparate series of abstract questions, which he will gradually learn to play with more or less ably. If he must study Spinoza, for example, he will have to make an enormous effort of memory to retain what Spinoza thought of God, causality, morals or emotions. The connection between all this is only a verbal sequence that leaves him cold. But sometimes, all of a sudden, a strange fire surges within him. Suddenly he becomes enflamed, he will be prepared to fight about such abstract questions as "substantial forms" or "synthetic *a priori* judgments." Suddenly, Aristotle, Spinoza and Kant become men in his eyes; he sees them as well-defined human types, or rather as simple attitudes around which the forms of speculation fall into place according to a living logic. Following the personal attitude he has adopted, he sees himself in a precise and well-defined relationship to each of these characters. He will cover one with insults, will make the other a god. For him, each will be a personal friend or enemy. Very quickly, having found the central secret, the simple and defined attitude that characterizes a Spinoza, he will know how to foresee, before having read, what Spinoza would think about a given problem. For him, the *Ethics* will stop being the forest primeval, for he will have discovered the hill from which the entire landscape spreads out before his eyes.

Every philosophy professor has noticed this phenomenon, almost each year, in one, two or three of the pupils in his class; but he can say nothing to produce it, nor to prevent it. At most, he can prepare the ground for it to bloom—not with verbal theories, but with the living example provided by his general attitude toward the world, himself and other men. This flame that, for an adolescent, suddenly colors the most arid forms of philosophical speculation, simultaneously engaging his thought, his passions and his actions—by which he will, for example, simultaneously and through a single internal act, be a Hegelian in philosophy, a Romantic in art, and a Socialist in politics—comes from a center in himself that is neither predominantly speculative activity, sensitivity nor discipline of action, but that illuminates these various functions in a single light. This flame is the search neither for true logic, nor the aesthetically beautiful, nor moral good, but for the Being that supports them, for what this Being is in its most irreplaceable essence. This flame is a question; but this question echoes in a desert. And most often, it is stifled. This little nascent fire, that should be protected and nourished like the most precious treasure, is drowned under a flood of words. It is crushed with metaphysics, whose answers, for lack of *Instructions for Use*, are illusory, ready-made sentiments, moral imperatives. When, still tiny, this question: "am I? and what am I?" begins to rumble in the young person, one should, as one does with a small child, nourish it carefully, with simple food in regulated quantities. One should tell this central questioner: "Begin by looking around you at your little domain, look at this machine of flesh you inhabit, learn to maneuver it, and see to what degree you depend on it. Look at how its enthusiasm and its disgust are aroused, transformed, quieted; how words and images link up and chain up your thought. And learn little by little to hold the reins of all these mechanisms." Instead, he is given the alcohol and rotten meat of dead theories; or else the real fruit of wisdom, without first being taught that he must break its skin. He is told about the Cosmos, God, Humanity, about everything except what is within his reach, what he can know and act upon: the little, specific, human construction that is part of his immediate world, one just as complete and more real at that moment than the great Universe.

General Philosophy should find its aim in the education of Being. Objectively, it should thus be realized in the education of man. And in fact, the wise men of old were educators, not indoctrinators. Pythagoras taught how to think, but also how to nourish. For there are means to provoke and to help the desire to be and to know, and there will always be a few people in the world who can apply them. But I do not wish to enter into that topic here. I want to remain at that final point where verbal philosophy, still manipulating words, uses speech to provoke men to surpass speech; at the point where, as Aristotle said, if we should not philosophize, we must still philosophize to prove that we shouldn't philosophize.

2. *The ambiguity of verbal expressions.*

This moment is the one at which a man, having acquired a certain knowledge, wants to convey it in words. First, in order to make it an object in the world, to give it a defined form, and thus to deliver himself completely from the problem he has just resolved. Second, so that others may benefit from this acquisition.

It hardly need be said that the very research which led to this knowledge cannot have been verbal. No verbal mechanisms can create truth. No true thought can be expressed in words if it has not been lived. But the constant use of spoken language in human relations engenders the illusion that language can of itself contain knowledge. If a stranger asks me for directions in the city where I live, I will tell him with the help of words. But he will only take this route if he already has a reason or a desire to go to such a place in the city. Now, since the beginning of time, men who have managed to live a certain knowledge have seen other men come to them asking for directions: those who had a goal and a desire to go received their directions and set out. But the majority stayed put, content to learn the master's explanations by heart, to adorn them with rhetoric, to put them into logical forms, and finally to draw maps. And by doing this, they imagined they were traveling. One, who had been a rich prince, the owner of a vast harem and many slaves, like Buddha in his youth, said to those who came to find him: "Pleasures and riches are vain and contemptible." And many, who had never tasted nor possessed anything, renounced what they did not have, denied themselves everything in order to find nothing; the master had made the entire journey of a human life and said, "I'll stop here." The others stopped even before they had left. Thus the naked expression of a piece of lived knowledge can lead the listener into the diametrically opposed error, if the listener does not first have the desire to know by living. Inversely, if the listener has this desire, two expressions using contradictory terms can lead him in identical fashion to pursue his goal. If he is a Christian, he can tell himself: "I have but one mortal life, thus I must strive toward my goal without wasting time." If he is a Buddhist, he will tell himself: "I will suffer from that which I failed to do today for many lives to come; thus I must at all moments strive to do what I do conscientiously, to avoid a perpetual and worsening repetition." But—more commonly, for man fears effort—the Christian will think: "God is so good...things will take care of themselves; and furthermore, my fate is already sealed"; and the Buddhist: "I have a thousand lives before me, I will always have the time..."

I have chosen my examples from the moral order because the ambivalence of its verbal expressions is flagrant. The double-edged nature of religious dogma comes from this ambivalence. Initially issuing from a real thought experienced in a human life, dogma is, for some, a stimulus to undergo a similar experience in their own lives. But for the majority, it is a haven for laziness, and the greater the authority of dogma in their eyes, the more they leave up to this dogma so as not to have to think or invent or search for themselves, since everything has already been found—by others! And in fact, the ambiguous nature of dogma—religious or otherwise—indicates that it is not only in the domain of morals that verbal expression threatens to stifle search. The same paradoxical cycle is pursued in the speculative domain. The more reality a thinker has put into his words, the more authority his words will have, and the more they will run the risk of becoming dogma that stifles doubt. And doubt is the motor of intellectual research. I know the story of a young man whom several fanatics wanted to make into a Messiah. The poor fellow never stopped proclaiming to the thousands who came to hear him: "Leave me! I can teach you nothing! Go away! Search for yourselves! It is at the base of his own life that each man must seek the truth." And the faithful said: "How true that is! Only a god can speak that way"; and they prostrated themselves all the more.

In this specific case, the inversion of values of a verbally correct formulation took a grotesque turn. But in the narrowest branch of teaching, the same problem occurs all the time to the professor or instructor: how to teach with words without the risk of having the formula taken for thought, or the rules of action for an accomplished fact? Luckily, in all the branches of teaching other than General Philosophy, we know that the language used does not contain its end in itself: we know, for example, that we will cure no illnesses by reciting a medical treatise as if it were a magic formula. But when General Philosophy is in question, it is as if the language used were an end in itself. In the best of cases, one adopts a cavalier attitude: if the pupil wants to know and experiment, he will find support and incitement in this language; if not, too bad. It is unfortunate that one must sometimes take this "too bad" literally, and run the risk of killing any real research under the blows of verbal "truths."

Every man who has thought, and tried to express the fruit of his thought, has attempted more or less successfully to resolve this problem. I would simply like to review some of the more effective means that have been found. I will not speak of the living example that these men, in their day, were able to provide for their students; only of what they sought to convey to posterity with words.[2]

Literally, "to convey" is false. In the richest library, there is not one atom of thought: only collections of typographical signs on sheets of paper. All that can be conveyed is a vessel for thought or a stimulus for the thinker; but whether or not the reader of a book has a thought to pour into this vessel or whether or not he reacts to the stimulus depends strictly on him.

3. The poetic image.

Some thinkers, understanding that the didactic formula ran the risk of being taken as an end in itself and that it could thus inhibit true research, were able to prevent this error by making the envelope of their thought *something finite but not final:* an end, not absolutely in itself, but an end in the sense that scholasticism speaks of "intermediate ends." In other words, they created works of art. Since we have limited our study to verbal expression, they became men of letters; and the greatest among them, poets.

The distinctive feature of poetry—not of "philosophical poetry," but of poetry worthy of this name, the creation of living thought—is that it is an object made of words, capable of suggesting, at the same time, physical images or bodily attitudes, feelings and ideas. It is thus a vessel suitable for receiving real,

2. I have limited this examination almost entirely to my encounters with Socrates and with several thinkers of ancient India, wanting to speak only from experience.

viable, form-endowed thought. He who, reading a poem, sees only the presentation of an idea, he who is satisfied with feeling it, or he who receives only a scene full of images, will have filled only part of the vessel with his thought; he will to some degree feel the incompleteness of the rest and will be inspired to seek the total meaning.

The expression of an experienced thought in poetic form should not be confused with aesthetic creation in the ordinary sense of the word. The artist generally aims at creating a work which would itself be its own end. It is true that such an artist is never found in his pure state, since he is always more or less mixed in with the moralist, political activist or philosopher. But to him, the concern with making something understood, in the full sense of the term, tends to be secondary; whereas it is the primary concern for the wise man when he expresses himself. I can admire Racine's poetry, I can marvel at its beauty, but this act of admiration does not involve my personal attitude toward the world and my life. I recognize, I feel and I perceive an expression which is true to its internal essence. But this truth is outside of me, and if this essence happens to be related to *my* essence, the author has nothing to do with it and this coincidence results from the order that governs my life, an order that he could not have foreseen.

On the contrary, the poem created by a thinker to give life, in a new body of words and images, to a truth he has experienced, involves my entire Being as soon as I agree to turn my attention to it. The aesthetic emotion will perhaps be less intense, perhaps almost nil, and yet this expression will be apt not only in relation to an external essence, but also with respect to an essence that permeates me. A simple formulation such as "One does not bathe twice in the same stream" already possesses this characteristic. There is, first, a perceptible image so simply expressed that I cannot escape its reality: a stream, a bather. This bather has a very defined attitude, which I cannot help but copy internally. He watches the water flow, always new and elusive. There is also a feeling—which goes from affliction to melancholy and later all the way to detachment—that I cannot avoid. It is imposed upon me. If I wish to free myself from it, I must use wiles, which are the beginnings of reflection. I tell myself: there is the word *stream*, but the formula is only true for *water*; but what is a stream without water? What remains if the substance of that stream is unseizable? A movement? In relation to what, to whom? To me? But why is this image and the idea it evokes bound to a feeling of sadness, a particular psychological state? Reciting this sentence, my face was looking slightly downward, my eyes were staring into the void, my body was immobile and relaxed. Only let me lift my eyes toward the sky, and this whole parade of images and words that the sentence provoked in me slows down and becomes blurred; let me make a violent physical effort, let me assume an angry attitude and it utterly vanishes. The formulation, then, only takes on its full meaning for a determiend vital attitude, which is manifested simultaneously in a physiological disposition, an emotional state, and a manner of thinking. It is this attitude, in return, that the poetic formulation *makes me understand* in its living totality. If someone had told me, "two phenomena, at two different times, cannot be identical, by virtue of the principle of imperceptibles; or else, by virtue of the principle of causality," I would have needed only a purely intellectual effort to understand; it would have given me no immediate knowledge of a real fact in my life. Whereas by telling me, across the centuries, that one does not bathe twice in the same stream, Heraclitus at once determines a defined attitude in the totality of my being. I know that we rarely make this effort to understand—which the author has not been able to make for us in advance—but we are wrong.

All of these wise men (I use this word, for want of one less faded, to avoid circumlocutions) have used this means—the poetic form—to give a durable effectiveness to the expression of their thought. It would be useless to multiply the examples: anyone can re-read the ancient Greek philosophers. In all of them, in Plato as well, even often in Aristotle, and in our philosophers at times, one will find these thought-vessels, able to contain a man from head to foot and to mold complete and defined vital actions.

Even more examples will be found in everyday language. Some of those expressions of wisdom, the fruit of thinkers who have left no name, have lasted longer than any monument and, in the form of proverbs and sayings, contribute one of the truest parts of our culture. Like the air we breathe, we do not know all that we owe to this treasure into which we dip every day. But these sayings can be passed on from mouth to mouth a thousand times and still go unheeded. Their meaning is only realized when a man pours his own thought into them. But whether or not man does this is a matter of chance, grace or freedom, as you like, but in any case of the unknown.

4. Images of Socrates and of everyone.

Several thinkers wanted to do more, to introduce into the words they handed over to humanity more direct inducements to really think — that is, to show, in all the force of this ridiculously over-used term, a certain presence. They wanted to avoid having their words taken for truth itself; and what's more, they wanted to prevent their words from being taken for mere works of art. There is something terribly dramatic — for whoever has tried to speak his mind — in the effort of a Plato, who used almost every possible means to destroy in his reader the illusion that his words by themselves contained truth, beauty and good. Still, we see philosophy manuals that present an overview of "Platonic philosophy" in several pages: as if, for a few francs and an hour of reading, anyone could possess the treasure that Socrates spent a life of hard labor to reach and communicate.

To convey the effectiveness of Socratic thought, Plato sought to convey to us the image of a man. And it is not his fault, but ours, if we read in his *Dialogues* only dialectical games or intellectual constructions. If we read, simply and conscientiously, a genuine man springs up before us, with his physical appearance, his humor, his ways of being; a man who, as soon as you have met him, stays with you. Socrates himself then becomes one of our familiar spirits. If I stray into easy abstractions, he is there to prove to me, with pitiless good humor, that the intellect by itself can affirm nothing real, that it only sets in motion possibilities, and often contradictory ones at that. It is the "head's" nature to be a Sophist, to fabricate vicious circles. What it can do, in the domain of real thought, is first to ask questions that it cannot resolve itself; then to inspire the rest, or rather all of Being, to seek the solution; and finally to guide man in his search. The wise men who govern the City are perhaps its essential element, but they alone will not form a city. Socrates' peculiar means of always calling attention back to real Being — that synthesis of Sage, Lion and Serpent — are:

1. *Intellectual contradiction*, or the art of the Sophist, reprehensible when it takes itself for an end, but which Socrates uses

in order to push man toward getting away from the contradiction through a vital act. This is why, at the end of the dialogue, he generally leaves the question hanging: "And now," he says, "let us go about our business." Which means: "Now that we have philosophized, let us go about understanding by living daily life."

2. *The use of complete symbols,* those related to all aspects of life and human thought: for example, the *State,* where from shoemaker to king, man—that is, you or me, Glaucon or Callicles—is described from head to foot. And the continual and insistent passage from the social to the individual prevents us from taking Socrates' discourses for a pure presentation of political ideas. The social symbol has the advantage of evoking an image that every man, in all the ages, will have before his eyes; of being consistent with itself and with man; and finally of being taken from a human reality which possesses its own laws, which we cannot fashion at will and which, consequently, keep us from straying. Thus do all the great human teachings call upon this symbol: the Kingdom of God, the Heavenly City of the Christians—the three primitive castes for the Hindus, which are the three "aspects" of man.[3] And this symbol, like any symbol grounded in life, is reversible, helping us to understand both the symbolizer and the symbolized. It is only in the modern age, an age of dissociation through loss of the single *center* of the thinking being, that symbols begin to live for themselves and that one sees the separate constitution of a psychology on one side, and a sociology on the other. Socrates is neither a psychologist nor a sociologist: he considers these two orders of existence under the single light of their essential analogy. The other symbols he puts into play are drawn from the world, the movements of stars or animals. Or else they are popular myths, those reservoirs of images crystallized by the centuries that are like the fundamental forms of real human thought: thought mixed and laden with emotion. Mythology

3. *Caste* in Sanskrit is *varna:* "color, aspect, way of seeing or describing"; the three primitive castes are (not *stem from,* as European translators usually write, but *are* in reality) the Head, the Arms (or the Chest) and the Thighs (the Stomach) of man (which the same translators, often for no reason, capitalize, or still more frequently do not translate at all, but leave in its Sanskrit form: *purusha).*

is the History of human histories. For each pagan god, when stripped of the modern "divine" and "supernatural" attributes in which we have clothed him, represents—on the stage of that vast theater which is a pantheon—a specific human type, brought to the highest degree of perfection in his particular aspect. He is thus more than existent. He is a concrete, universal form of human existence. When we classify or try to define, practically, the human types around us, images such as those of Don Quixote, Harpagon, or Père Ubu are more help to us than any abstract concept: they are actually concrete general categories. The characters of ancient mythology differ from these literary types only in their greater generality; certain among them are even universal types, well-tried by secular use, which in disguised forms still serve us daily when we think of our fellow men.

This characteristic of mythological creations already separates them from a purely verbal expression. And yet words, when a poet uses them, can give rise to images. With words, the poet can provoke in the reader a *form* of thought endowed with all the attributes of human existence, and thus inspire him not only to formulate concepts, but also to feel and make dance within himself the general attitude or behavior of a defined human state.

On the one hand, Socrates condemned scholarly mythological creations, dead and absurd allegories forged from a concept and a verbal expression, images made of juxtaposed fragments having only a conceptual and verbal link. But on the other hand, he openly accepted *every* creation of popular mythology: living creations, subject not to a verbal logic, but to a vital logic. Socrates' alternating condemnation and acceptance of the gods has often been seen as contradiction, or as sarcasm, or as debater's opportunism. In reality, he condemns the allegory that is but the imagistic clothing of an abstraction, in order to accept the "god" *created* and *nourished* by the thought of peoples: image given life by an internal necessity, common to all men. And this makes it *"immortal."* It is only by a secondary reflection that *to nourish* a god came to be understood as "to worship" him, and that his real "immortality" (just as relative as the durability of the human species) became an abstract "immortality." Thus mythology becomes theology; and those myths *consubstantial* with man are shrouded in mystery, rite and metaphysical speculation, all of which finally rob us of them.

5. Several Hindu Socrates.

Every man who has wished to convey a lived knowledge to his fellows has used images latent in the collective thought of his time. He has revived the gods in man and, as a result, has very often entered into conflict with the theology of his time. This fact is remarkably highlighted in the Hindu *Upanishads* which, because of the problem of *conveyance of knowledge* posed therein and of the means by which this problem is resolved, greatly resemble the Socratic dialogues. As these resemblances are not due, it seems, to historical influence, but rather originate in the same concern for *conveying knowledge whose verbal expression does not run the danger of becoming an end in itself*, presenting them could be a useful means of clarifying our subject.

1. *The dialogue form* is frequent in the *Upanishads*. The abundance (as in Plato) of exclamatory and expletive particles[4] ("isn't it?... for sure... but of course!... Oh, no!... well then...," etc.); the sober but lively notations of the dialogue's scene and characters;[5] all those elements, finally, that most translators neglect as accessories demonstrate a constant concern for showing *men thinking*, and not abstract thoughts.

2. *Intellectual contradiction* is so constant in the *Upanishads* that Hindu speculation was able to draw six doctrines from these texts, or rather six different "aspects" *(darshana)*, sometimes contradictory, but all six considered orthodox. The discussions with contradictory theses in the *Upanishads* are introduced, as in Plato, by the staging of several interlocutors who are questioned by the master. For example, five theologians come to find a famous master, and the discussion centers around the "being who is common to all men." All five, when questioned, define this being as a metaphysical "substance": for one it is the Sky, for the others the Sun, the Wind, Space, the Oceans, the Earth. The master listens to their definitions and tells them (I am abridging somewhat): "Yes, it is true that the Sky is common to all men, in other words that all men have a head. But if you

---

4. *u, uta, evam, vai, bā, khila, kalu, hi, ha, atha, anga,* etc.

5. For example: "It was under a cart, scratching his scabs, that he found him, and he slipped in beside him..." (For these examples and those which follow, I have limited myself to the *Chāndogyopanishad* — which has not been contaminated by modern reworkings — to avoid being submerged in the wealth of documents.)

make this the absolute Being, it means that you have a life of the head. That is all well and good, but it is not enough; and if you continue to be all head, the head will explode..." And so on, up to the fifth, to whom he declares: "The Earth, you say? In other words, that on which we stand; in other words, the feet, and the material basis of your life. It is because you wish to have a firm earthly position, rich herds of cattle, etc. That's all well and good, but it is not enough; furthermore, if you continue to be all feet, your feet will lose their strength." We see here the desire to reduce verbal philosophy by contradiction, to make one pass from the theological point of view — that is, cosmological or ontological, general, abstract and external — to the point of view of the genuine, specific man: the being common to all men is not a given general entity, nor even "man in general," but the living totality, the irreplaceable solitude of each man.[6] Or, as it is stated more simply in the same dialogue: "Man must speak only of the goal that makes him live."

3. *The constant reference to a living symbol* (which can itself be taken as a secondary aim of the discussion). As we saw in the *Republic*, social symbols have the privilege of being both *tangible* and *complete* (that is, linked to man's totality: activity, affectivity, representation), and of being, relative to an individual's life, very durable; they will then remain a direct language for all individuals of the same civilization and for the entire duration of this form of civilization. The most frequent symbolism in the *Upanishads* is that of sacrifice — essentially, of *keeping a fire burning*. As this sacred act is the center not only of Hindu civilization, but perhaps of every ancient civilization, I will return to it in greater detail.

6. *Word rechargers.*

There is another, very durable social reality, one common to many individuals, that can serve as a basis for extra-verbal teaching: it is the very *imagery* of language, distinct from its purely logical function. Science and logic, for their own ends, need to empty words as much as possible of their motor or emotional content and of their metaphorical meanings. It is clear

---

6. "[the *brahman* (the Word)] is thus considered under a double aspect (*adishtam*): that which concerns oneself (*adhyātmam*) and that which concerns the manifestation (*adhidevatam*)."

that when we speak, in geometry, of a "triangle inscribed within a circle," it is better for us not to think of a "triple anguish engraved in the heart of something that turns," which would be etymologically exact. In the extreme case, the language of logic becomes algebra and logistics, completely stripped of images. In this latter state, it hardly runs the risk of being taken for knowledge in itself. But the illusion persists in the intermediate forms of abstract language when we speak of "mind," "body," "God," "matter," and so on. Philosophical language arranges these words according to the schematic residues that remain in them after one has negated the images, vital attitudes and sentiments that constituted their original foundation. The role of this abstraction is not to make one think, but *to predict what one will think* WHEN *one thinks*. Relieved of their images, words are like the forms of objects that the artist can derive from matter, and they are no longer subject to the same conditions of time and space as thoughts and real objects. One can move them much faster, which explains the terrible: *Meliora video proboque, deteriora sequor.* For I, the follower, am not an abstract word; I am weighed down by a body. The philosopher is a cartographer of human life. In the same way that the cartographer, having extracted the contours of a country from its geological substance, can reduce this form to whatever dimensions he likes and reproduce it on a small sheet of paper, so the philosopher, in a short space of time, can logically dispose of the general forms of existence that would perhaps require years for him to explore. If it is well done, his discourse will surely help him in his voyage, and will help his fellow men. Discursive philosophy is as necessary to knowledge as the geographical map is to travel. The great error, I repeat, is to believe that one can travel by looking at a map.

When the problem of incitement to travel is posed, we can indeed wonder: is it possible to use a geographical map not only to guide, but also to provoke the trip? In any case, it is the most we can do, for the map will never, as far as I'm concerned, make the effort necessary to start me on the road. We must seek the answer from those concerned: in other words, travel agents and transport companies. The answer is that one can, among other means, use the geological map, in the form of a poster, to incite people to travel. But then it becomes necessary to embellish it with images: one will perhaps neglect geographical exactitude, painting a palm tree and a camel on Africa, a Roman ruin on Italy, and so forth. In other words, one reintegrates into the abstract schemas, in the form of images, some of the physical reality from which it has been torn.

To keep to the two examples I have chosen, we know the use Socrates made of etymology. Analogous procedures are found in all the literature connected with the Veda. Sanskrit, in which each of the several thousand monosyllabic roots has a concrete meaning that is almost always directly recognizable, lends itself marvelously well to these exercises. Comparisons of words according to voicing, or etymology, use of the same word, in the same text, with different meanings—all of this E. Senart called "philosophy by puns." This is true, except for the pejorative connotations of the word "pun." I do not believe we can make a precise distinction between an "etymology" and a "pun." Etymological "truth" is extremely elusive. If I am told that the words *léguer* (to bequeath) and *legs* (legacy) have no etymological kinship, this teaches me nothing useful. As long as the word *legs* is written with a *g*, it is a new word, which really is related to *léguer.* Only the scholar can create false etymologies. The common man, on the other hand, as soon as he brings two words together, actually links them, and from then on, those words are united by a new connection like two trees grafted together. There are, in truth—in the *Cratylus,* for example, or in the glossaries of the Vedas—learned etymologies, no more or less exact than ours, which can serve as mnemonic devices (in the Vedic glossaries, this is, it seems, their main role). But when, in the dialogues of the *Upanishads,* the speakers take words apart and put them back together, join them in new ways and present them under various angles, they in no way do it in the vain hope of finding an impossible "etymological truth." They do it for two major reasons:

1. First, to charge the word with a power which is simultaneously motor, emotional and representative, in order to create, between it and living man, the most varied relations, involving him in a real act and inciting him to get away from purely verbal knowledge. I will take yet another example, among hundreds, from the *Upanishad* I quoted above, intended for the "Singers of Hymns." The word for hymn is *sāman.* The concrete ties of this word seem to have been, in the time of the Vedas, already fairly remote: it was associated with ideas of "lowing"

and "propitiation," but its very special liturgical use had made it almost purely technical. It is this word which gives the Third Veda (the one in which the songs are written melodically) its title. In order to restore the word's direct human value, to remind the cantor that the hymn he was called upon to sing was not a mechanical ritual act, but a veritable operation on himself, this is what was explained to him:

Sāma (nominative *neuter* of *sāman)* is composed of *sā:* "she, her"; and of *āma:* "he, him"—two elements that are in the female's relation to the male. "She"—that is, she who spreads out before our eyes, who is female, a fertile but not fertilizing substance—is the Earth. "He," the male, the driving force that creates nothing by itself but without which the Earth's productions would remain inert, is Fire—domestic fire which is the soul of the hearth, or vital fire, animal heat that distinguishes the living being from the corpse. The *sāman,* neutral in gender, is the union of Earth and Fire, of the body and life. Then, in the same way, *sā* (she) and *āma* (he) are respectively identified with pairs: Atmosphere-Wind; Sky-Sun; Constellations-Moon; White Light (perceived as being spread out) and minuscule Black Hole of the eye's pupil (it is the unspread blackness that perceives and penetrates the female light); word and breath (breath is male, for, non-sonorous, this is what gives sound to words, its females); Eye and Self (that is, sight and the seer); Hearing and Feeling (through which we perceive melodic forms). And through a whole series of analogies, "he" and "she" are identified with the dual aspect of every manifestation. Finally, this cosmological view is explicitly related to a direct vision of man himself. When the cantor pronounces the *sāman,* it is a marriage that he must perform between his body (Earth), his affectivity (Atmosphere), his thought (Sky), and the "Himself" (*ātman)* that is *simultaneously* the heat of this body, the force of this affectivity, and the sun of this thought. This is why he is a sacred cantor, and not an opera singer. A little further on, the same word, *sāman,* is explained differently,[7] proving once and for all that the text is not aiming toward an "etymology," but toward a vivification of the word.

7. Still elsewhere, *sāman* is compared to the root *so, sā,* "tear, destroy; finish off"; the *sāman* is that which destroys illusions and, musically, completes the meaning of the stanza.

2. Speculations on words have still another meaning in the *Upanishads*. They are linked to the fact that the dialogues are presented as models of real dialogue, and not as literary artifice. So we see what each of us can notice in our own conversations: that the same word can have different *meanings*, and particularly different, often contradictory *values*, for different individuals. Thus the word *ātman* (initially "breath, breath of life, life, *anima*, then *animus*," and finally "the person," "oneself") is the source of enormous confusion, because each understands it as the thing he is used to identifying with: body, passions, feelings, imagination, intellect, will—the exact same confusion that modern readers of Plato can have about the "know *yourself*."

When language is pushed this way, thought can no longer be satisfied with the support of words. It must leap from them to seek its resolutions elsewhere. This "elsewhere" must not be understood as a transcendental plane, a mysterious metaphysical realm; this "elsewhere" is "here," in the immediacy of real life. It is from *here* that our thought leaves, and it is *here* that it must return; but after such detours! First live, then philosophize; but third, live again. Plato's man in the cave must leave the cave, contemplate the sun's light and, *armed with this light* which he keeps in his memory, go back into the cave. Verbal philosophy is but a necessary stage of the journey.

7. The value of discourse in traditional knowledge.

I insist on recalling here, to clarify what I said above about Hindu speculation, how this human journey was not only socially conceived, but also organized and instituted in the ancient civilization of India.

The foundation of this civilization is the *Veda*. The basis of the Veda is a collection of hymns which are considered extremely obscure. The truth is that *our minds* are obscured before their essential simplicity: we let ourselves be dazzled by the astounding wealth of metaphors, and we lose sight of the ever-simple fact described by these luminous images—a fact so simple that one would have to become a little child once again in order to understand it. I can only give this approximation:

Man cannot live without fire; and you cannot build a fire without burning something.

This, for lack of a better summary, is the center of the Veda's teaching. The brahman acquires this teaching during the four stages of his life:

1. In his seventeenth year, the child enters social life. He learns by heart (and by head) the hymns of the Veda; he learns to sing of every aspect of the fire which gives men life, the heat emitted by this fire, the combustible substance which feeds the fire. Rhythms, melodies and ritual gestures are inscribed in his body, and will serve him throughout his life as a measure of all things.

2. Between the ages of twenty and thirty, in general, the young man marries and becomes master of a household. It is during this period that he actively participates in social life. He has finished studying the Hymns; now he must read the commentaries on these hymns, called *Brāhmanas*. The general meaning of these commentaries is liturgical and mythological. The original teachings of the *Vedas* are, in substance, developed in this way:

"This Fire, if it gives men life, is thus a powerful deity; and since it cannot manifest itself to us unless we give it food, we must offer it sacrifices. Let us then adore the Fire; let us also adore the Heat which spreads everywhere, even when the fire has disappeared, and which therefore is still a powerful god. Let us adore the Sun, which is celestial Fire. Let us adore the flammable liquid which is used to revive the Fire, father of the Fire which gives us life, and which is thus our ancestor. Let us also adore the ancestors...," and thus, by successive metaphors, from a simple primitive *observation*, a whole mythology and complicated ritual develop. This tangle of metaphors and logical deductions must be pushed by man all the way to its final consequences; and even if he has already re-discovered the simple and original meaning at the base of this mythology, he must continue to make sacrifices and speak of the gods—for his present function is above all to provide a living for his family and raise his children. He must therefore be able to answer, using the right metaphors—that is, metaphors which are linked to real things—the questions his children will ask him (for children then were already asking their parents the same questions as today): "Where does this fire go when it goes out? What is it saying when it crackles? Who is its father? Does the Sun's fire also eat wood? Who lit the Sun? by rubbing which sticks?..." To the child who sees in each thing a *person*, it would be premature to give scientific or metaphysical explanations; but it would be still more dangerous to tell him just anything about those *persons*. There are true myths and false myths. The myths of the *Brahmanas* were true in the sense that their "gods" maintained relations identical, as relations to those that unite the physical elements of fire, combustible matter, smoke, heat; of the sun, clouds, dawn, light; relations identical, finally, to those that unite the elements with the activities of the little world that is man. This solid system of analogies, founded on physical fact, will serve the child's animist thought; and it will remain valid when man, turning his gaze away from the outside world, turns it toward the inner one.

3. The inward turning of the gaze becomes explicit in the third phase of life according to Hindu tradition. The master of the house, "when he sees his children's children before him," has completed his task. He may then "go off into the forest."[8] He takes with him the *Forest Books*, which are commentaries on the *same* hymns of the Veda. These books tell him: "This fire which gives you life is not the physical fire which burned in your home: it is the internal fire which animates your body and your thoughts; it is the active principle of yourself. It is to this fire that you must offer sacrifice, and the fuel it asks is your own substance. All the gods you adored, which designate your faculties, your activities and your ways of being, are creations of language." Man then begins to weave in himself the same network of analogies that theology established among the "gods."

4. Finally, when he has built and contemplated his internal world, he is ripe for a fourth teaching (which is still another commentary on the *same* hymns): that of the *Upanishads*—that is, according to the Hindu explanation of the word, the teaching which cuts through illusion. All that he thought he knew, they tell him, is but words. The Veda itself is but words. The "gods" he has nourished within himself are but words, with no reality other than that which man himself confers upon them—if this man *is*. But to speak of this last state would be pure verbiage.

8. "When the master of the house sees his wrinkles and white hair, and his offspring's offspring, then let him go take refuge in the forest... Having disseminated the 'Offering of the Protector of Progeny' and given everything prescribed by the Knowledge, then gathering the Fires in himself, let the brāhman wander from his home" (*Laws of Manu*, VI, 2, 38).

All that man can then say, upon returning from the "forest" (forest which is itself often metaphorical), are the Veda's original words, in their simplicity: man cannot live without fire, and you cannot build a fire without burning something. There is no longer any need to adorn these words with theology or metaphysics. He can again sing the verses of the Veda as he sang them in childhood—the same words, but whose meaning has been nourished, developed, then absorbed and consummated by an entire lifetime of experience. This is what the Hindus mean by the word *vedānta*, which designates the end, the basis, the last word and, at the same time, the consummation of traditional knowledge.

The existence of a traditional knowledge is what allowed ancient India to represent, even in its social institutions, the normal course—or what *should* be the normal course—of human life: from ignorant simplicity to conscious and recreated simplicity, passing through the complexity of a search embracing all of life's manifestations. It is because words were intimately linked to this architecture of life that Hindu verbal speculation still maintains its relative and transitory character as the intermediary between the *question* from which it springs and the *solution* into which it must disappear.

I have chosen the Hindu tradition as my example because it has made every possible effort to leave behind verbal documents that cannot be understood through purely verbal speculation.* We would find analogous characteristics (in the precise sense of the term) in the Judeo-Christian tradition—for example, in the cabbalistic texts, which also go up to the limit of the expressible. But when speaking of traditions still too related to our forms of culture, we risk angering the exegetes and confusing everything. Nonetheless, I considered it useful to show the profound analogies between Socratic testimony and those of the *Upanishads*. These comparisons can help a Westerner become familiar with Hindu thought, which is ordinarily buried under a jumble of

The manuscript reads: "The advantage of the Vedic tradition is that all the interpretations able to be expressed by the written word have been set down in books; thus all that I have claimed is verifiable and I am sure to have interpreted nothing according to whim." [French editor's note.]

sometimes knowledgeable, sometimes sentimental ramblings.[9]

At the same time, I hope that this summary of what traditional knowledge is will show that the absence of such knowledge goes hand in hand with the existence of *verbal philosophies that are taken as ends in themselves.* But we cannot recreate traditional knowledge, embracing all human thought and activity, from scratch. Nor can we imitate a foreign tradition or revive a dead one; for a people as for individuals, one man's law can be deadly for another. Still, the analogy of Hindu tradition can suggest to us that traditional knowledge must always be erected on the basis of a collective myth, linked to institutions and maintaining concrete relations with nature and society. At present, I see only scientific knowledge, linked to technological development and modern economic evolution, as conforming somewhat to this definition: *that* is what mythology is, and not the literary genre one usually calls by this name. It is difficult for us to conceive of our technical knowledge as "myth," so much do we identify with it. But the "myths" of the ancients were no more "mythical" for them. Whatever the "myth" in which we are steeped, General Philosophy, the search for Being, will not be able to consummate it unless it breaks out of its own verbal limitations. But at that point, it will have to be carried out in a direct work of human culture, in a new, *actual* harmony between Nature, economic organization, institutions, various bodies of knowledge, arts and sciences, and man's basic needs.

And if that is a dream, well then! let us awaken.

(1934.)

9. *Knowledgeable ramblings:* according to Benfey and Haug, the word *brāhman* initially designated "the little whisk made of *kusa* grass (Poa cynosuroides?) that was passed from hand to hand during the sacrifice." Furthermore, according to Haug, the word *veda* also referred to the same little whisk (Haug, *Le Sens primitif du mot Brahma* [The original meaning of the word "Brahma"], 1868, p. 4).

ON THE LIFE OF BASILES

The sectioned ones.

Tibetan legend tells of a singularly appalling monster. Reading about it fills your mouth with a block of salt. This creature, larva or demon, generally has a human shape. From afar, you would think it was a lost traveler or sleepwalker. But as this thing comes closer, you see that its head, limbs and trunk float in the air, barely held together by rather loose threads. The worst thing, the unpardonable thing, is that this horror suffers and wants to live. These human pieces come toward you, ask you for drink or food; but you feel only bottomless fear and revulsion. You sense the danger of contagion. Deep down, you feel you could become one of these larvae. And out of fear, you loathe it.

Old wives' tales! We cultivated souls, free of the shadows of superstition, know very well that man, that marvel of creation, is a harmonious and homogenous whole; that we are little walking and admirably organized republics; that each of us is an individual unique in his kind; in other words, that we can sleep soundly and reject these morbid fantasies of an ignorant people.

And then again, no! Just look—these piecemeal monsters fill the streets. Look at them, and especially let us look at ourselves. All of us, to some degree, resemble these sectioned things. With one, the heart has its reasons that reason doesn't know, the head is hungry when the belly is full; with another, the intellect wears itself out in vicious circles while the decapitated body attends to daily needs. And each one in his own way, a way he is often proud of, is thus cut up in pieces barely held together by the loose threads of social function or of an obscure animal desire to live.

Lucky people, Tibetan though it may be, if it considers these creatures exceptional and legendary! For us, on the contrary, it is the coherent man, made of a solid block, who would clash, crash and amaze. Take a good look, and you will see only hordes of dismembered phantoms who suffer, and who are our brothers.

Basile.

Still, this sectioned thing does not always disintegrate completely. We see it maintain a kind of individuality for years on end. What keeps the pieces together? What causes me, when I remember having swum or drunk a glass of water, felt fear or anger, read a book or counted the number of nails in a door, to claim that I am the one who did or experienced these actions or these emotions which have no possible point of reference among them? Who in me continually proclaims, straight-faced, puns such as: "I hate this poem," and "I hate calf sweetbread"? Who is the "liaison officer"?

It is a certain Basile. Man created him in his image, unless it's the other way around. But he is no larger than a louse or, more proverbially, than a mite, so that in the human body where he resides he can only be in one place at a time.

The pataphysics of Basile.

Up until now, Basile has eluded the most acute scientific investigations. This is why: in the living subject, it is highly improbable (even if, denying him any kind of initiative, one wishes to submit him entirely to the statistical laws currently in vogue), it is almost impossible, then, that he will happen to be, at a given time, in the exact spot the scientist is examining. Furthermore, under X-ray analysis, even with the most modern methods for studying slides, one would be hard put to distinguish him from a blood clot or minuscule concretion; even then, it is doubtful that he would show up on an X-ray; and finally, his extreme mobility prevents any photography. In the corpse, he is nowhere to be found. Whether he is reabsorbed at the moment of decease or whether he clears out (and to what shelter), no one has the slightest idea—least of all himself, it seems.

But we who practice the pataphysical method called experimentation by the absurd, state: if you deny Basile, Basile will deny you. And you will run a serious risk of falling apart altogether.

Aspects of Basile.

While he always keeps his general human shape, Basile is quite prone to taking on the form of the part of the body in which he happens to be at a given moment. In the skull, he becomes macrocephalic; in the belly, paunchy; in the hands, claw-like or even tentacular, and so on. But as he generally has his choice spot, he gradually takes on a permanent deformation. In return, this deformation makes the other areas quite uncomfortable for him, and he is often loath to leave the abode in which he has taken root and shape. And if he occasionally makes hesitant excursions, he always returns to his lair for rest and food.

So it is that the Basiles—our dear Basiles—differ from one another. Roughly, we can separate them into three categories, according to their conformation and their habitat:

> the Paunchine Basiles,
> the Torsine Basiles,
> and the Cerebriate Basiles.

Those of the first category strongly resemble Père Ubu or, in an order of size closer to reality, the well-fed flea, the tick called "book louse," or the chigger after several weeks of being embedded in a well-irrigated dermis. Their tiny heads have the chitinous toughness of the cockchafer larva's, and serve the same ventral function. But contrary to the future beetle, it does not aim, even unconsciously, toward metamorphosis. Other quite common varieties are similar to aegypans, satyrs, fauns or capricorn beetles, minus the horns. Still others combine the dryad and the ubu, without attaining the serenity of the Egyptian cynocephalus. But what good is it to list what everyone sees parading every day before his eyes?

The Torsine Basiles often resemble pigeons, peacocks, cocks, all sorts of birds, especially the kind that puffs out its throat and swells its breastbone. Like them as well, they can live a fairly long time without the appearance of excessive dysfunctions, once the cerebral hemispheres have been properly removed. Others are leonine, quick to strike or to lick, and already Socrates said how, with a little care, we could "make good watch dogs out of them." We find Torsine Basiles, for example, in career army officers and apostolic souls; and, affected by certain illnesses of languor, in a fair number of lyric poets.

Cerebriate Basiles, finally, have the form of tadpoles. For the most part, they live in representatives of *Intelligenzias*. If ever they cross over the throat that separates their home from the other regions, they can sow great disorder in the latter; as can, furthermore, any kind of Basile that ventures out of his adopted place.

(But you must come out, Basile, you will come out, Basile, you will come out of that hole.)

The language of Basiles.

All these Basiles, dissimilar as they may be and wherever they may be found, use the same language. But each of them understands it in his own way; hence misunderstandings and confusion. And far from creating a Pentecost, this linguistic ambiguity turns more often into Babel. One day, at a café, I heard three Basiles—a Paunchine, a Torsine and a Cerebriate, in fact—hidden in three persons of human countenance, three good friends, and speaking through the latters' mouths. They had come to an agreement on the maximal assertion that "research and love of truth should guide all their conduct." This was pure Basile. And just as one hears quite differently in Greek than in French the schoolboy joke: *"Où qu'est la bonne Pauline...,"** so it was necessary to translate the words of these three Basiles into a Christian tongue:

(Cerebriate Basile, in lingua barbara): *"Quod est verum, hoc est desirabile. Mea autem propositio est vera. Ergo propositio mea est desirabilis.* Yes, but one cannot desire what one already possesses. *Ergo seu propositio mea non est mea, seu falsa est.* But enough thinking, logistics will get us out of this one."

(Torsine Basile, in good French): "Sacred love of Countree-e-e!"

(Paunchine Basile, in the language of experts): "I love a good sausage."

As it was dinner time, it was the latter who put the greatest emphasis into his words. And all hugs and kisses (they were on their fifth aperitif), out of love for truth and country, they went off to eat sausage, and other things. The three Basiles set-

---

*The "schoolboy joke" consists of replacing a phrase in Ancient Greek, for example, with a similar-sounding but unrelated phrase in French. The example given above translates: "Wherever good old Pauline is..."

tled into their respective stomachs. Then the communion of bellies was celebrated, and they were brothers. After the liqueurs, Cerebrate Basile went back up to his skull. He was sleepy, and rested comfortably only in that spot. Near the famous second left frontal convolution, he got tangled up in the folds of a banderole on which he happened to read: "Science has no country." And pulling at it, he set off—perhaps involuntarily—the vocal mechanism of his man, who uttered: "Science has no country."

Torsine Basile, who had gone up to take a nap in his mediastinum, heard this and retorted: "My dear fellow, I was in the war, I'll have you know, and..." he was off, and continued until he was red, white and blue in the face. Paunchine Basile, worried about his digestion, made it known by the guy he was inside that he wanted "peace and quiet." He was called a pacifist and a defeatist by Torsine Basile, while Cerebrate accused them both of being "simple minds." They were on the point of coming to blows (not the Basiles, but their men), when someone cried out: "Fire! Fire!" The three Basiles hastily descended toward the buttocks, settled in behind the control panels of the hind legs and set them hopping. Harmony was restored by the communion of legs and fire in the behind, as one sees wolf and doe flee side by side from a burning forest.

The consciousness of Basile.

It is a weary, dreary and wandering consciousness, a paltry glow-worm's light that scarcely manages to warm the little nook of man to which it is attached, a sickly flame, subject to all outside drafts. Sometimes the breath of a word or a passing shape revives it for an instant. But unable to find sufficient fuel at home, when no outside breeze blows strong enough to revive it without being so violent as to put it out, it drags on and languishes, so pale and slow that if not for its mobility, one would take it for a fungus. Sometimes, however, the following happens:

Here we would need the great trumpet of Judgment, we would need to swing the heavens like bells to ring out the miracle's coming, ring loud and long so that the worlds can prepare to see it—and then silence! and look through the royal gateway. Here is the dramatic turn of events.

Basile remembers that his name comes from the Greek and

means "king," or at very least, "kingly." And that "all will be forgiven man, except forgetting that he is the son of a king."

Basile, suddenly roused (he must have received a good blow on the head, or something like that), sees himself deformed, macrocephalic, hump-backed, obese, or a legless cripple. Poor king! and unhappy kingdom! The fields, neglected or abandoned to greedy industry, produce too much here and too little there. Wild beasts ravage the flocks; the harvests rot because the king, pushed by the ambition of an over-zealous heart, was waging external war or else because he spent his time in feasts and debaucheries. Or else barbarians oppress his people because he did nothing but dream on the palace balconies about the stars. Sorry palace! disorder and injustice are everywhere. Basile awakened makes himself leave the chambers—harem, banquet hall or observatory—in which he had confined himself for so long. He visits his dwelling from attic to basement. He crosses through that whole moving and laborious mass of flesh, bone, skin, blood, nerves, those feet, those hands, that mouth and those windows open on the outside world. He inspects his subjects, questions them on their desires: are they hungry, and for what? bread? images? thoughts? Everywhere he finds halls piled with scrap furniture, unemptied garbage pails, cobwebs and old newspapers. He must tidy and clean here, fill in and repair there. Tear down these old worm-eaten scaffoldings made, with the least possible effort, of self-love or chatter, pasted over with painted cardboard—and rebuild. Basile, king, this living abode of flesh is your Basilica. In the crypts of your Basilica, Basile, lives your worst enemy, the Basilisk. For years, out of laziness, you have let him get fat on your substance, and he has even stolen your name. He is a multiform hydra whose look changes everything to stone. Under the Basilisk's glance, appetites become manias, desires vices, thoughts syllogisms, and the living house of man becomes a rigid tomb.

Basile spits out flames, send thunderbolts crashing and drenches everything in flammable liquid: mortal splendor for the Basilisk who responds with streams of venom. It will be a long war.

Basile rebuilds his Basilica. He does not know if he will live long enough to bring his work to fruition. But never again does he want to fall into negligence, and it is not for love of this life that he would live to be a hundred.

The immense very-small.

In the back of a closet, Basile found several dusty books which, for a change, he didn't burn. Strangely enough, the words in these books were combined in such a way that they made sense only to him, Basile, to the very center of the awakened Basile. For the head alone, for the thorax alone, for the belly alone, they are only disconcerting and tiresome insanities. In one of these books, for example, he read:

"In this body, citadel of the Utterer, is a little calyx, a residence. Inside this, a little space. Within this is what you must seek, yes, *this* is what you must wish to know... As vast as the space spread outside of us is, so this space within the heart is vast. Sky and Earth are united there, Fire and Wind, Sun and Moon, Lightning and Stars, all that one has and all that one does not have here: all of that is united... This being within my heart is smaller than a grain of rice, than a grain of barley, than a mustard seed, than a millet seed, than the germ of a millet seed. This being within my heart is greater than the great Earth, greater than the Atmosphere, greater than the luminous Sky, greater than all the worlds... That minuteness is the living essence of all things; it is real Being; it is the self: you are that!..."

Basile understood that they meant *him*, that he *was* not yet. The book was called *Teachings for the Singers of Rhythms*, and whether it came from the star Sirius, from Belgium or from New Guinea, Basile cared little.   •   •

The torments of Cerebriate Basile.

I will now speak of the torments of the Cerebriate Basiles; not that the others are less worthy of interest, far from it. But whereas Reader Basile and Author Basile probably belong to the Cerebriate category, they will have a greater chance of understanding each other on this terrain of grey matter. Nonetheless, or rather *thus*, this hope is purely theoretical; and it is somewhat blindly that these two Basiles, by the often illusory intermediary of printed signs, try to make contact.

Physmathics Basile, having split the atom and successively separated its electrons, its ions, its neutrons and its deutrons, splashes about in a magma of undulating corpuscles, sparks of energy and elusive *quanta* subject to the laws of heads-or-tails. The limits of his universe flee from him at a speed which is not even constant. The good old Euclidian and mechanistic crutches abandon him, and he finds no other support.

111

Philosopher Basile is unable to supply him with one, as by rights he should: he has been completely dazed by his search for the "concrete," as he says to designate the most abstract of philosophical abstractions. He hopes that by blaring and ringing "concrete! concrete! concrete!" he really will create or find or understand a real, fully real thing or fact. One of his latest finds was to describe "the living content" of his mental operations; one of these days, I warn him, he will notice that it is not the content but the container that lives, that shapes the content as in a mold. But again he will forget that Cerebriate's head must perfect the rest of the body before the adult animal can contain, understand, hold and feel in his internal palms the slightest living reality. In the meantime, he continues to empty words like "real," "life" and "concrete" of their content – like all the others that pass through his mouth, by virtue of mechanical repetition, as everyone has had the opportunity to experience. If words are bullets, Philosopher is shooting blanks. Arteest Basile, for his part, wears a little smirk of superiority. At least *he* handles matter. He says that it's no longer an age for lyrical diarrhea (good news, at any rate), and that *he* has a trade, ideas, feelings, and everything. But if we were to ask him what he does with all that, and why – but ask him eye to eye, a knife at his throat to shove all his ready-made and parroting answers back down – then you will see him make the face of a whale, or a snail, to whom one asks an embarrassing question; or else he will admit to worries that have nothing to do with building the Basilica.

The most inveterate of fat-headed Basiles agree on this point: they are caught in vicious circles. They no longer have a firm vision of the world which could guide their lives; they have lost contact with other Basiles, with Everyman Basile, Off-the-Street Basile, Earth Basile, Factory Basile – as well as with their own bodies, and with their own lives.

Prosopopeia of a Basile.

"I regret," said Egomet Basile suddenly, interrupting me in mid-sentence, "having to speak in the first person. It is a last resort. This is my story. A childhood without religious upbringing put me prematurely face to face with the fear of death. It was, as I finally realized, a tightening in the pit of my stomach, which a simple relaxation of the abdominal muscles could dispel. Thus I freed myself from this stomach-fear, but the tightening went up into the chest in the form of a knot of dread. The same observation and the same work of relaxation dispelled this throat-fear. And the tightening went further up into the brain in the form of a problem: to be or not to be—a question which is worn out, but rarely thought out. This tightening, then, turned over and over in my brain, and remained there for a good number of years. It proliferated in metaphysical speculations and almost resulted in complete decapitation. My head is still congested, but I had a few strokes of luck that will perhaps allow me to turn it to my advantage.

"I sought the answer to the unformulated question in the philosophers, then in the sages and the great writings not signed by men's names. I found double-edged myths and algebras. One could use them to rock oneself into a peaceful slumber, full of sweet dreams, of tomorrows, of 'sufficient unto the day'; but also to note that one had understood nothing *today,* and to try to understand things *otherwise.* I began to look for this 'otherwise' in my rare moments of activity."

Professional secrets.

He continued: "I believed for some time that poetic activity—as I made the guy I was inside say—putting the totality of man into play, would be enough for my life. I was to become disenchanted, so to speak. I am in a good position to say here, and too bad if I betray the brotherhood, that the literary exercise we now call 'poetry' is over nine-tenths shameless bluff, masquerades, ignorance of everything (of language, of the weight and life of words and images, and of ideas if there are any; of the trade, of the means; and especially of the ends), of irresponsibility, of vanity, of self-love in its ten-million ramifications, and of laziness—that is, made of multi-faceted nothingness, absences, hollows veiled by vague mirages. If this were not so, it would indeed be a possible way. It would even be the only way, but at that point it would no longer be a literary exercise."

De re publica.

"In public matters, I didn't last very long. The same sectioning that I noticed in the individual I also saw in society, with all it entails in surpluses and shortages, in degeneracy of the privileged and the exploiters, and in degradation of the exploited and starving. I hoped to establish contact with the human masses. I initially believed that relations were falsified by the intermediaries (more Cerebrate creatures and creations) that I wished to use. No: it was in me, as in each of us, that the relations were false. The contact must be reestablished one day, but *other* than by means of the head; when that happens, it will really be something."

Meetings.

"Thus I had to clean out the Basilica, throw out the useless books, and try to fit in. But how? With all that 'I must...I must...,' I could have stayed years, a whole lifetime, a vain lifetime, a life of *ifs*... and *tomorrows*..., a life in the future and the conditional.

"I met a human being. I wouldn't have believed it possible. And yet I was forced to abandon some very handy despair. *Hope* is the hardest thing to bear.

"A short time later, in another part of the world—travel brings about such meetings when one is not traveling to escape—I met the person who bears my name: a psychic pulp shut up inside a human skin, in which various chunks of varied materials floated, some still usable, some rather precious, and much to be completely replaced.

"If I told you that after this I met still another human being, you would accuse me of writing a serial novel. So I won't talk about it. I will simply tell you this: that in a little town in Europe, someone organizes meetings between Basiles and their men. I do not know what the others do there, it's their business. *I*, Basile, meet the guy I'm inside; he and I are often curiously surprised. How little we know each other, and we thought we were such old pals! We get to know each other again, we put down our masks one by one, and we are far from having finished! We argue and make up. I know I must sound like a drunkard to speak like this about something so simple. It *is* simple—but this word is harder to take than one would think." Basile suddenly stopped talking, rapped me sharply on the mouth and said curtly: "Enough, chatterbox!"

(And yet it was *he* who was talking! And *I* am the one he accuses of chattering. How unfair!)

(1934-35.)

114

BETWEEN TWO STOOLS

I sent Hermès, *a review in Brussels that was publishing a very interesting issue on the relation between poetry and magic, the following letter. Having considered the two words "poetry" and "magic" from all angles, I tried to endow them with their most useful and elevated meanings. At the same time, I granted the editorial committee permission to publish my letter; but it wasn't used because, they wrote, my "note was not in line with the aims of this issue." From which you can judge, after reading my letter, in what realm* Hermès' *research is situated. Personally, I find it quite a strange realm, in which the discourse on the object is more important than the object itself—despite the collaboration, as the table of contents shows, of men for whom thinking is not a luxury. Should one speak of things one has experienced, or should one speak in order to be spared experience? It certainly puts the nature and destiny of Western speculative thought in doubt.*

Five or six years ago, I would have answered your request with several rather pathetic, rather well-documented, rather brilliant pages. I thought I knew so many things. Since then, I've had to face reality and have vomited up my poor little semblance of knowledge. Now I know that I know nothing, so to speak. No longer knowing, but not yet having attained knowledge, my butt between two stools: tell me, is that a position from which to expound?

No, but it is a good position from which to see what is really important, to learn how to be silent, and to work at relearning speech. This already touches on your particular subject, and this is how it appears to me from the uncomfortable position in which I find myself.

First of all, then, what is really important? I would like to put *your* backs against the wall, a knife at your throats, and have you answer first. Don't try to answer with words, it's impossible. Then, having decided what is important, let us see what use the magic of words and poetry could be. If you want to understand what I'm going to say next, stop reading for a minute (but take me literally), and during this minute observe how and why you begin to formulate answers or objections to my questions.

Have you finished? Let's go on. *Thus,* we must first stand more clearly and more simply in the center of our universe, and to do this, among other means of cleaning house, we must be silent. When I say "be silent," I mean more than simply to stop talking. When I say "the day," I mean more than the absence of night; I also mean that the sun is rising.

And now, learn how to speak again. Not (as people often mean by the word magic) to make rain fall, or to make someone love you, or to make an enemy drop dead, or to make the listener cry: all that hardly differs, in essence, from the power of the words with which you have someone bring you a drink in a café. These are always somewhat difficult, somewhat banal techniques, but they only pursue secondary aims. What kind of word-magic can serve the nameless end? Perhaps speech is an excretion and, as excretion puts an end to digestion and allows us to assimilate food, speech would thus be a way of emptying outselves in order to fill up again, in other words to be silent. And thus speech and silence would alternate like day and night, under the unchanging eye of the single Sun, their father. But the comparison between speech and excretion would stop, on the one hand, at the fact that the first is edible, and on the other that speech comes out from above, for it is the crown of experience. But how many stolen crowns adorn phantom kings!

To write any more would be illusory verbiage; twice illusory, for writing is not speaking. Your subject is too close to me for me to hesitate in telling you: literary contact, through the medium of the printed word, among collaborators or between author and reader, is by itself incomplete. It lacks the essential, which can only be aroused by working in common toward resolving (and not only by means of the head) a question which is just as common to all as it is specific to each one. I would not, even if I had the presumption to think I could, want to discourage you; quite the contrary. But beware of literature, beware of philosophy, beware of imaginary voyages, beware of vicarious experience, beware of things that don't commit you to anything, to anything essential. And remember that one does not move one's body by means of a treatise on anatomy, but out of a desire to move and with a goal in sight; and so it is with speech. And that one does not perceive a sound by means of another sound, but through hearing; in the same way one does not know speech by means of words, but through silence.

(1936.)

THE POWERS OF THE WORD IN HINDU POETICS[1]

A Hindu invention.

Toward the beginning of our age, it is said, an anonymous resident of India invented a marvelous tool. It was immaterial but representable, its specific characteristic was to exist only figuratively and, in the history of our civilization, it has played perhaps a greater role than the steam engine or the microscope. In the eight or ten centuries that followed, wherever Hindu influence extended, from Ceylon to Mongolia, from Pendjas to Bali, the use of this tool—which is essentially nothing—spread. This instrument, which Greek science had lacked, largely helped the Arabs to become the learned people of the Middle Ages. The Arabs popularized it in North Africa and Europe and, if the object itself is Hindu, we still call it by its Arab name. No day goes by in which we do not use this instrument made

1. For the most part, this study is a summary, which I would like to be at least as faithful as a literal translation, of some of the most important Sanskrit texts on the art of poetry, and particularly of (I will refer to these works by their initials):

   (S.D.) Sāhitya Darpana (V. note 7); having excluded the parts strictly relevant to dramatic composition;

   (A.P.) Agni Purāna, adhyāyās 336ff.;

   (N.S.) Natya-Shāstra, adhy. I, VI, XVII.

   I apologize for being obliged, because of the importance of exact terminology, to use many Sanskrit nouns, transcribed according to convention. The reader will avoid the most common errors of pronunciation by reading *c* as "ch," *j* as "dj," *h* always aspirate, *u* as "oo" (in "tool"), *e* as long "a" (as in "they"), *o* always long, *a* as in "father," and *ams* with a nasal sound, as in the French *"anse."* Capitalized English words should be read as technical terms.

   I have not tried to translate quotes from the Sanskrit poems given as examples; the reader will find in his own language, in the poets he enjoys, examples which are much more convincing than necessarily imperfect translations [slightly revised note].

   Quotations from the *S.D.* are loosely based on the English translation by Pramada-Dasa Mitra (Calcutta: Baptist Mission Press, 1875).—Trans.

of nothing, this sign meaning nothing, this little circle (Arab writing reduces it to a dot) called the zero.

Numeration being a specific case of language, a singularly perfect and precise language, the invention of the zero—along with its correlative, the positional value of digits—lets us infer the specific effort of Hindu genius in all the linguistic arts. What, then, is the power of the zero?—simply to signify *the passage to a new order of magnitude*. When I have exhausted the series of digits (from 1 to 9 in our number system), I draw a little circle signifying that this series is finished and that the digits I am going to write immediately to the left of the little circle, although of the same shape, will represent numbers in another order of magnitude: tens, and so on. The circular figure that serves to note the zero means that it is both emptiness and plenitude: it is the emptiness resulting from the completion of a cycle. Thus the series of Indo-Arabic digits is written from 1 to 0, and not from 0 to 9.[2]

We will see how the Hindus seek analagous processes of passage to higher degrees of meaning in verbal language as well.

2. The Sanskrit name for the zero is *kha*, which also means: hole, orifice (in the body: sensory organ), emptiness, dot, infinite space, sky, air; specifically, it is the hub of a wheel, the immobile center which makes rotation possible (the wheel itself would be more illustrative of Chinese genius: "It is the emptiness at the center that allows for use of the wheel," says Lao-tse). *Kha* is also happiness, knowledge, activity, and the *brahman* itself (in these three aspects), the immobile motor, also called *ka*, the *"Quod?" (Chāndogya Up.*, IV, 10, 5). Through the game of synonyms, the zero is also called "sky" (*ambara, vyoman*) or "infinite" (*ananata*): every number being a limitation of the unnumbered.

Instead of writing a number in digits, the authors of technical treatises often prefer to name the digits successively, beginning with units (thus going backward with respect to writing), by means of metaphorical expressions. Thus 1,320 will be written: *"infinite (= 0), eye (= 2), fire (= 3,* for each master of the house keeps three fires burning), *moon (= 1)";* or again: *"sky (= 0), tooth (= 32), ace (= 1,* in dice)." Here, the words "infinite" or "sky" warn us that the following nouns, "eye" or "tooth," will mean tens—that is, 20 or 320, and not 2 or 32.

119

The Vedic epoch.

In the *Veda*,[3] the linguistic arts already have an eminent position. Of the six annexed sciences essential to the study of the *Veda*, four directly concern language: Phonetics, Grammar, Lexicology and Metrics. But we could not dissociate them from the two others, Ritual and Astronomy, no more than from liturgical Music and Dance, the Architecture of the altar, Physiopsychology, Jurisprudence or Politics. All these branches of knowledge were integrated in a single body of doctrine and served a single end. It would thus be vain, and furthermore absurd, to speak of a "Vedic poetics" without having at least a passing knowledge of the Vedic tradition in its entirety.

I will merely cite a habit of Vedic language. In it we apprehend a process which, in the domain of words, is analogous to the one invented centuries later, in the realm of digits: the comparison by negation, commonly used in hymns. To say, for example, "immovable as a mountain," the Vedic first says "mountain." Then, to make the word pass from the physical to the analogical sense, he nullifies the first meaning by following the word with its negation: "mountain-*not* immovable," he says. And in the same way (word for word): "arrow-*not* on the bow is placed thought"; that is: "like an arrow..."; or if you prefer: "arrow? no, on the bow thought has been placed"—the word "bow," like "arrow," undergoing a similar transposition by negation.[4] To say "arrow-not" to signify "like an arrow," or to write 40, "four-zero," to signify "four tens," are two parallel procedures.

---

3. The *Veda*, in the general sense, comprises: I. Four collections of poems (the *Vedas*), subdivided into *mantra* (hymns or ritual expressions), *brāhmana* (treatises on sacrifice), *āranyaka* ("the forest books": internal sacrifice), *upanishad* (the doctrine itself).—II. The six *vedānga* (cited in the text).—III. The four *upaveda* (applied sciences: medicine, martial arts, music, architecture). There is no science or technique, in India, which has not been related to this corpus of traditional doctrine; each can serve as a means of access to the sacred teaching, and orthodox treatises have been written on commercial art, eroticism, thievery and, as we will see, aesthetics. (On the *Veda*, v. Max Müller, *The Origin and Growth of Religion.*)

4. Here are the two examples quoted above: *parvato na acyutah (R.V., I, 52, 2); ishur na dhanvan prati dhīyate matih (R.V., IX, 69, 1)*. Note that *na* has a "positional value"; placed before the word, it would take back its properly negative function.

The aim of art.

With the passing of the centuries, the Vedic language evolved. Regions and dialects developed. Secular arts and sciences grew around the sacred knowledge. In schools devoted to maintaining the tradition, men were concerned with fixing the language before time and the influence of Dravidian speech patterns could change it beyond recognition. They reworked it, codified it, rebuilt it on the laws of analogy. They classified vocal sounds according to a chart which, in large part, we still use today. They determined – all the while limiting – the phonetic changes that words would undergo in a sentence. They drew up catalogues of roots, analyzed the value of inflection, set up rules of derivation and composition. In short, they created *Sanskrit*– that is, the "well-crafted," "perfected" or "consecrated" tongue, as far removed from the *prākrits* or "natural speech" as the latter are removed from animal cries.[5]

The same effort was made to resist the invasion of the secular sciences. To prevent heresy, they grouped specific aspects of the single doctrine into six "ways of seeing" (*shad-darshana*), true in their relation to each other, despite certain apparent contradictions. Finally, they considered reconstructing the secular arts themselves from a traditional framework; these secular arts would thus become garments and vehicles for the old teachings, the bridge between the sacred and the profane.

The aim of art is clearly defined in the first chapter of the *Treatise on Theater* by Bharata, the oldest and highest Hindu authority on matters of aesthetics.[6] We read there that Brahma,

5. *Samskrta(m)* – of which the old transcription, "sanscrutan," gave a better idea of the real pronunciation – would indeed mean "artificial," without the pejorative value attached to this word. As an adjective, when applied to a man, it can mean "perfected" by the sacraments (*samskāra*) of rebirth, and designate the "twice-born" *(dvija)*. The word *prākrta* means "produced by *prakrti*" (Nature, in the widest sense). Sanskrit was definitively codified in the work of Panini (6th or 5th century B.C.), to whom modern linguistics owes much of its progress.

6. In the October 15, 1935, issue of *Mesures*, I published an annotated translation of this first chapter of the *N.S. (The Origin of Theater)*. The theater is called "visible Poetry," in contrast to "[only] audible Poetry," to which I have limited the present study. *Kāvya*, "poetry" and *kavi*, "poet" also mean "wisdom, wise" from the root *kū, kav,* "to sing," or from *ku,* "to direct one's thought." [English translations of some of Daumal's writings on Hindu theater can be found in R. Daumal, *Rasa* (L.L. Levi, trans.); New York: New Directions, 1982. – trans.]

121

to make the sacred teachings accessible "even to the servile caste," invented the Theater, total art, "extracted from the substance of the four Vedas...founded on the law of the interconnection of acts and states."

"I have made this Theater," declares Brahmā himself",...so that it can describe the manifestations of this Threefold World in its entirety... I modeled this Theater on the movement of the universe... For sacred Knowledge, science and myth it will provide a place to be heard, and for the crowds, amusement: such will this Theater be" (*N.S.*, I, 12 to 16, 104 to 119).

We find the same concept in a classical treatise on Poetry, the "Mirror of Composition" (*S.D.*),[7] much more recent but following the same tradition, which will serve as our guide in this study:

"Poetry is a means of attaining the four great objects of human desire [*artha*, material goods; *Kāma*, pleasure-pain, attraction-repulsion; *dharma*, good-evil, knowledge of the law; finally, *moksha*, desire for deliverance, effort to free oneself from the preceding motives]... The attainment of these four objects, such as one finds them in the sacred Books, by reason of their dryness, can only be grasped with the greatest effort, even by those whose intelligence is fully mature. Whereas poetry, by reason of its producing a fund of highest delight, makes this search pleasant even to those whose intelligence is still in its infancy. —But then, someone will object, since the sacred Books exist, why should men of mature minds bother with Poetry? —This is not a valid objection; for, if it were found that a disease, curable with bitter medicines, could also be cured with sugar candy, who then, afflicted with this disease, would

7. *Sāhitya-Darpana*, by Vishvanātha Kavirāja. The author is said to have been "minister of war and peace" under a king of Bengal at a very unspecified time (between the 12th and 16th centuries). There is perhaps an allusion to his political life in this poem, which is presented in his work simply as an example of a certain stylistic figure: "For the water of generosity: desert sands; for the depiction of great deeds: wall of air; for the moonlight of virtue: fourteenth day of waning; for rightness: elegance of a dog's tail. —Those who out of mad hope have served that line of kings of the Black Age: what skill they will need to serve the Trident-Carrier [Shiva], which only love can let them reach!" See *Nature essentielle de la Poésie* [The essential nature of Poetry] (chapt. I of the *S.D.*) in the review *Présence;* Geneva, May 1935.

not prefer treatment by sugar candy?... The aim of Poetry is to offer a savor to be tasted, as one would offer a sweet; and in this way, to teach those whose intelligence is still in infancy...that they must behave like Rāma and his fellows, and not like Rāvana and his fellows and, more generally, that one must or must not act in a given manner..." (*S.D.*, I, 2).

We should not take this last sentence, nor the examples of the hero Rāma and the savage Rāvana with ten faces, as a lowering of Poetry to a stupidly moralizing role: the context of the entire Hindu tradition forbids it. Orientals have no concept of the "categorical imperative";[8] after the advice or command, we must always understand: "*if* one wishes to reach a given goal"—a goal which, here, is liberation. Furthermore, we will see that the important thing, in this definition of the aim of Poetry, is "a savor to be tasted," and that this expression must be given a very precise meaning.

The essence of Poetry.

For, before examining the procedures by which language passes from one level of meaning to another, we must define, according to Hindu aesthetics, the highest level of meaning the language of words can attain, that which confers upon the word the title of Poetry.

The author of the *S.D.* begins by refuting several definitions

8. This pseudo-notion, furthermore, is non-existent outside of so-called philosophy manuals and classes. For Kant himself, there was basically only one categorical imperative: "act as the legislator of your own universe," which leads to the dilemma: be free or be a slave. The aim of Poetry is not to hold Rāma up as an example while saying "do as he does" (we will see that this would go against the very definition of Poetry), but to make the listener experience Rāma, to transform him gradually and truly into a Rāma; whereas moral literature only teaches one to ape real or imaginary virtues. P. Masson-Oursel clearly recognized the reason for representing heroes: "the exaltation of a splendid example through recreation in the self" ("L'esthétique indienne," in *Revue de Métaphysique et de Morale*, 1936, no. 3).

which others have given of Poetry[9]: neither the appropriateness of meaning with respect to sound, nor perfect possession of language, nor capable use of figures, nor a mastery of the various "movements" of style, nor the "power to suggest" are enough to make Poetry. All of this confers *qualities* on Poetry, which are more or less necessary to it. But "the *essence* is absolutely removed from that... What then, in the final account, is Poetry? To this we reply: *Poetry is a sentence whose essence is Savor (Vākyam rasātmakam kāvyam)*...Savor is the very reality, the life of Poetry...*Savor (rasa,* from the root *ras,* to taste) means: that which is savored, tasted (*rasyate)" (S.D.,* I, 3).* By Savor, we mean (to summarize the definitions given by the various treatises) the moment of consciousness that the veritable work of art must bring about in whoever is "gifted with internal Being" and "who has a measure to judge by."[10] The symbol of Savor is clear: first,

9. Like the "six aspects" of orthodox doctrine, the various schools of Hindu aesthetics, which are all related to the work of Bharata (the *N.S.* is called the "fifth Veda"), are differing points of view more than opposing systems. Roughly, we could classify them according to the notions that occupy the primary position in each of them (the following terms will be defined in the course of this article): *alamkāra, rīti, dhvani, rasa.* The latter school, that of Savor, is the most fertile: the principle treatises on dramatic and poetic art come from this school. The doctrine of the *Agni Purāna* (chap. 36ff.) is related to it, despite its eclecticism; also that of Bhoja—somewhat peculiar, it is true, in that it subordinates all Savors to the Erotic. The recent discovery of the *N.S.* manuscripts gave this school new vigor. The *S.D.,* in fact, reconciles the apparent opposition between the *dhvani* school ("Resonance, or Suggestion, is the essence of Poetry") and the *rasa* school ("Savor is the essence of Poetry") by accepting the second definition, but granting the *dhvani* an indispensable role in the evocation of *rasa.*
Rasa, translated here as "Savor," has been rendered variously as "Flavor," "Taste," or "Relish" in different translations of the *S.D.*

10. "What we call the Luminous Principle is the state of thought which is not affected by [the two other principles of] Passion and Darkness." In other words, the three *guna* or fundamental principles of all existence in Hindu psycho-cosmology: *tamas,* darkness, inertia, passivity, downward tendency, tendency toward mechanical repetition; *rajas,* intermediate force, passion, expansive force, conceived of as the colored, the red, between the two other principles which are black and white, and (this is one of the most ancient meanings) as the atmosphere, region of winds and clouds, between moon and sky; *sattva,* luminous, active principle, upward tendency, toward Being *(sat),* principle of intelligence;

"this principle emerges, becomes present, when it has surmounted the two others" (Commentary).

All that is subject to the laws of these three principles is considered "natural" (*prākrta*, production of *prakrti*). Savor is "supra-natural"; but only when the appropriate hierarchy has been established between the three natural principles – particularly when thought, whose function is to manifest *sattva*, has taken the lead position – can Savor appear. By the same token, we see what an error it would be to follow the all-too-common interpretation of *rasa* as "emotion." "*Supernatural Wonder*" (*camatkāra*), origin of all the specific Savors (Dharmadatta, quoted in *S.D.*, III, 33), is actually not the feeling of stupor and evidence (of "enlargement," *vistāra*) one feels when contemplating a creation conforming to one's idea, but a state of the togetherness of all Being which includes this feeling: like three schoolboys who were fighting among themselves, the three *guna* suddenly made peace and rushed back to their assigned seats upon the master's entry.

"Gifted with internal Being": *sahrdaya*, literally "who has a heart." But the heart, or rather (in this case) the smallest cavity of the heart (*hrdaya*), is not the seat of emotions for the Hindus; it's the individual's "full and immobile" center, the residence of the "master of the city" (*pura*), of "Man" (*purusha*). (*Chāndogya Up.*, III, 12, 9; VIII, 1. *Katha Up.*, II, 3, 17; etc.)

"Who has a measure to judge by, an internal measure": *pramātr*, "commensurator," so to speak; more precisely, he who is able to recreate in himself the *laws of form* or *pramāna*. These laws are represented in the plastic arts by the traditional canons. In logic, the same *pramāna* designate a proof, a criterion of truth: they always concern the activity of thought becoming aware of a form by reconstructing it, by concording with this form which has been presented to it (in one case as a tangible figure, in the other as a logical proposition). So it is that knowledge of the circle as circle is identical to the operation of ideally drawing the circle. This notion deserves further development, which space does not allow here. On this subject, v. P. Masson-Oursel, *art. cit.* and *Une connexion entre l'esthetique et la philosophie de l'Inde, la notion de prāmana* [A connection between Indian aesthetics and philosophy: the notion of *prāmana*], in *Revue des Arts asiatiques*, II, 1925. Also A.K. Coomaraswamy, *Introduction to the Art of Eastern Asia* (Boston Museum and Madras), and other works. In general, the works of these two authors are, to my mind (and this is much more thanks than judgment), the best written in a European language on Indian aesthetics (v. the bibliography given in the volume *L'Inde antique*, in the series *Evolution de l'humanite*; Renaissance du Livre, 1933).

Metaphysically, Savor would come from the "absolute Joy" (*ānanda*) aspect of *brahman* (whose other two aspects are "Being," *sat*, and "Knowledge," *cit*) (*A.P.*). The "Joy" we are discussing here has, of course, nothing to do with any pleasant emotion.

a savor is immediately perceived; second, among all our senses, taste is peculiar in that the object must be introduced into the body to be tasted; and finally, as the physical organism is tasting a substance, it already begins to assimilate it into its own substance. But we must be careful not to be waylaid by certain superficially similar metaphors that exist in our own tongues, such as "artistic taste," "flavorful language." Savor, in the higher and more general meaning given it by the Hindus, is even quite above art:

> "Appearing concurrently with the Luminous Principle, indivisible, self-manifested, made of Joy and Thought united, free from contact with other perceptions, twin sister of the *brahman's* gustation, the life of which is supernatural Wonder: such is Savor, which those who have a measure to judge by enjoy as the true, inseparable form of the self" (*S.D.*, III, 33).

Savor is the direct and distinctive perception of a particular state *(bhava)* that is characterized, in the arts, by a dominant sentiment. Thus, for Savor to exist, one must experience a feeling and at the same time distinguish oneself from it; in other words, one must become conscious of it: "Because it is essentially knowledge, Savor is said to be shining in its own evidence" *(S.D.*, III, 60). It is simple, like the flavor of a dish made of various ingredients (*N.S.*, VI, 32). It is joy, but joy that doesn't depend on the contingencies of ordinary life; active joy, which doesn't stop being joy even when it springs from the representation of painful objects.[11] It is "supernatural, supraphysical" *(lokottara)* or "unworldly" *(alaukika)*, in that it is neither sensation, emotion, nor concept.

11. "Even in a Savor such as the Pathetic, a superior kind of joy is produced... It is true that all things which produce sorrow, pleasure, etc., when they have their mooring in this world, bring about sorrows, pleasures, etc., in worldly fashion. But when they have reached a level of representation transcending this world, and have their mooring in Poetry, all these causes produce only joy" (*S.D.*, III, 35, 37). In this we recognize an application to individual psychology of the doctrine of the *purusha*, which is not affected by the modifications of its envelopes (v. René Guénon, *L'Homme et son devenir selon le Vedanta*, et al.; this would, furthermore, be the best introduction to the metaphysical aspect of Hindu tradition). We see how much the theory of *rasa* surpasses "art-as-catharsis" theories, and puts them in their place.

"It is not an entity existing independently of its perception, which one would make appear as one makes a jug appear by shining a lamp on it. And, as the author of the *Locana* [The *Eye* of Poetry] says: 'to say that one tastes Savor is like saying that one cooks pilaf [which, strictly speaking, is improper: pilaf does not exist before the rice is cooked; nor Savor outside of its being tasted]... It is neither past, nor future, nor persistent' [as an object persists even if it is not perceived]...'" (*S.D.*, III, 54-57).

It is or it is not: such is the formulation hidden behind these negative definitions.

To be tasted, Savor requires from the listener (or the spectator) the "internal representation" of the states manifesting it, and active "participation" in what is being represented.[12] Only by having the experience proposed by the poet will he reach the moment of "tasting himself," which is the essence of Poetry.

12. "Gustation is not produced without the internal represenation (*vāsanā*) of the states [evoked by the poet]. And Dharmadatta said: 'In the theater, those spectators who are capable of Representation can taste Savor, but those who do not have the faculty of Representation are like the beams, the walls and the stones.'" We must no doubt understand the word *vāsanā*, following the *Yoga*, as "that which subsists" of an action, either as a memory or as a lasting modification of the individual, who through this becomes able to understand what he had previously experienced.

"The evocation of states by the representation of their causes, etc., has an operation called the 'making common' (*sādhārani krtih*). By virtue of this, the listener competent to appreciate Poetry makes himself out to be indistinct from the hero [in a given unusual situation suggested by the poet], as for example, he jumps across the sea...; in such a way that he no longer says to himself: that is the other's and this is mine" (*S.D.*, III, 39 to 43). *Making common does not mean to be confused with:* as he actively participates in the poem, the listener removes himself from his own emotions and becomes their spectator. Thus, in the case of theater, the relations between *actor, character* and *audience* are clarified: "the moment the actor realizes the poem's meaning, he shows in his own person the hero's essential form, simultaneously putting himself in the position of spectator" *(ibid.);* thus the spectator experiences himself as the hero of the drama, the actor as the spectator, and it's the hero (that is, in the final account, the poet's thought) who is the actor.

Savors and their manifestations.

However, "Savor" is not synonymous with the moment of awakening to oneself: the word designates such a moment only when it springs from the representation of a state dominated by a sentiment. It is this use of sentiment as intermediary that defines Poetry in general, whereas works such as the *Upanishads,* which are addressed primarily to the intelligence, are said to be "without Savor" *(nīrasa).* It follows, in practice, that Savor is differentiated into a certain number of specific "Savors" that correspond to the principal sentiments liable to animate the poem. The oldest texts recognize eight Savors, four of them fundamental: Erotic, Furious, Heroic, Horrible; and four that are given as their respective passive aspects: Comic, Pathetic, Marvelous, Terrible (*N.S.*, VI, 39ff.).[13] Often they add the Savor called Peaceful (calm arising from the taming of passions) and sometimes the Savor corresponding to maternal or paternal love.

Savor is to its manifestations *(bhāva)* what the flavor of a dish is to the substances composing it. Savor and Manifestation condition each other in the poem; "there is no Savor without Manifestation, no Manifestation without Savor." But their relation is hierarchical: "As the seed comes from the tree, and from the tree the flower and the fruit, so all Savors are the roots from which the Manifestations spring" (*N.S.*, VI, 36, 38). Thus, there are 8, or 9, or 10 "principle sentiments," manifested in turn by the representation of their *causes* ("substantial" causes:

13. The meaning of this classification must have changed. We can still understand, without forcing the meanings of words too much, that terror, marvel and pathos are respectively effects of the Horrible, the Heroic and the Furious; we don't quite see how the Comic would be an "imitation of the Erotic" (*N.S.*, VI, 39ff.). Most likely, all these terms originally had a more systematic and more intelligible meaning. The name of the first Savor, *shringāra* (which I've translated, as is customary, by "Erotic," the only advantage being that it is somewhat ambiguous), is especially bizarre: "by *horn (shringa)* we signify the shock [or "the bursting"] of amorous passion (literally, "of that which makes [hearts] churn"); and *shringāra* is *what is caused by that [horn]..."* (*S.D.*, III, 209); the corresponding sentiment, love *(rati),* is defined as "a sentimental inclination toward an object favorable to this sentiment [that is, able to nourish it]" (207). A color and a divinity is attributed to each Savor (*N.S.*, VI, 42-44): through these symbolic references, perhaps, we could get some idea of the original system.

characters/supports of these sentiments, or "enhancing" causes: actions, objects, etc., occasional causes of sentiments); of their *effects* (particularly physiological); and of their *passing accompaniments*. These classifications, of which this is but a brief summary, were especially developed for the theater. They form the psychological keyboard on which the actor-dancer, stage director, musician or poet play; they open a wide field of improvisation to the latter and, in so doing, free them.[14]

The body of Poetry.

To provoke these manifestations in the audience, the poet has at his command the language of words, the material of Poetry. "Sound and sense united constitute the body of Poetry" *(Dhvani,* quoted in *S.D.,* I, 2).

The sounds of the voice (*varna,* phonemes) are combined into vocables (*shabda*). The union of a vocable and a sense *(artha)* produces a word *(pada).*[15] *"The word is an assemblage of letters— or at times a single letter—equipped for grammatical usage* (this excludes pure roots and grammatical themes), *without a logical connection between them* (this excludes compounds acting as propositions, a process peculiar to Sanskrit), *conveying one meaning* ("aeiou" are five vowels; they don't mean anything; they do not form a word), *and only one meaning" (S.D.,* II). This last

14. Example: a sub-variety of amorous passion is that in which the lovers have not yet met in private *(pūrvarāga).* Ask an actor to make up a list of clear and characteristic signs of this sentiment, which he could convey by his acting. Hindu classification proposes ten, each of which immediately suggests others, and which could, furthermore, manifest three different qualities of passion. Has your actor found as many?

15. The two terms *shabda* and *pada* are generally translated indifferently as "word," which strips Hindu theory of all its meaning. We could suggest better English equivalents than "vocable" and "word," but it is indispensable that we maintain the distinction. As for *artha,* it signifies "thing, object, aim, motive, usefulness"; thus, if you will, the "thing" (or the "image" of the thing) in contrast to its name, but still more the "aim" of the word, the "motive" of the person using it and the benefit (the "Fruit," *phala,* the Hindus also say) that one will reap from it. In English, "sense" must retain its etymological duality (double aspect of a single meaning) of "signification" and "direction" (cf. the Old English root *sith,* "journey," or the French *sens)* [slightly revised note].

condition is worth examining. The same vocable can be joined to several successive meanings, but not simultaneously. Each time a new word results. A word that is no longer distinctly understood falls back to the level of vocable. We will see that this requirement of a single meaning for each word – as, despite all appearances, the meaning of the word "sense"– is precisely the motor which makes the language pass from one degree of signification to another.

Thus, there can be no isolated words. It is only in their current use, in the *sentence,* that vocables can act as words.

> *"The sentence (vākya) is an assembly of words possessing: compatibility*("he irrigates with fire" is not a sentence), *expectancy* ([a subject calling for a verb or an attribute, etc.]: "cow horse man elephant" is not a sentence) *and proximity* (in perception; to say "Theodore" one day, and the next day [when you have forgotten] "walks," is not a sentence)... Strictly speaking, "expectancy" and "proximity" respectively belong to [the thought of] the person [who is speaking or listening] and to meaning; it is only figuratively that they are taken here as "properties of the sentence" *(S.D., II).*

Thus, just as there are no words outside of the sentence, there are no sentences outside of the speaker's intention and the listener's perception. Hindu linguistics never forgot that all language simultaneously supposed a common language, a meaning or aim of speech, a speaker *(vaktr),* and a listener who hears *(boddhr).*

The union of sound and sense, then, constitutes "the body of Poetry." The term used here, *sharīra,* designates the body, in the *Vedānta,* as "that which is divisible and dissolvable"; not exclusively the physical body, but the totality of Man's "envelopes." Thus, we must not be surprised to hear the "body" of Poetry used not only for the phonetic material (timbres, articulations, tones and durations), but also for the meaning, or rather the hierarchy of meanings of which vocal sounds form the vulgar envelope. We will see how this analogy of the poem and man is developed: the body of the poem will have its "movements" *(rīti)* determined by attitudes *(samsthā),* it will wear "ornaments" and be subject to "faults" or disabilities; while the "self" *(ātman)* of the poem will be manifested by "merits" *(guna) (S.D.,* I, 2, quoting the *Dhvani).*

The "three powers" of language.

A vocable can serve as vehicle for all kinds of meanings *(S.D., II)*:

1. *The literal meaning* is that of the dictionary; the vocable carrying it then carries out the function of "designation" *(abhidā)*. There are four categories of vocable, according to whether they literally designate a *genus* (e.g., "cow"), a *quality* (or specific difference, e.g., "white [cow]"), a *substance* (or singular object, e.g., *"Vishnu'*) or an *action* (done or suffered, accident of a substance, e.g., "cooking").

2. *The figurative meaning* (I am using this term for the sake of convenience, but we will understand it according to the meaning about to be defined) arises from an incompatibility between the vocable's literal meaning and the context (e.g., "I smoke filters," where "I smoke" prevents "filters" from taking on its literal meaning); the vocable then carries out the function of "representation" *(lakshana)*. The new meaning, which comes from the negation of the literal one, reestablishes both the unity of meaning without which there would be no word, and the compatibility of words without which there would be no sentence: now we see the importance of these two conditions in the definitions of word and sentence.

The passage to the figurative sense can be:

Conventional or *motivated:* in "I smoke filters," the meaning of "filter cigarettes" is represented by "filters," by virtue of linguistic *convention*. But I can say "the frock coats entered," using "frock coats" to represent "men wearing frock coats," my *motive* being to show, for example, the obsolete and somewhat ridiculous solemnity of the scene I am describing;

Inclusive or *non-inclusive* of the literal meaning: in the first case, the literal meaning is preserved, as a quality, for example, of the figurative sense (as in the preceding example, in which the literal "frock coats" remains a belonging of the represented "men"); in the second case, the literal sense completely disappears (as in the first example);

Explicitly indicated or *understood*, according to whether the figurative sense does or does not cover a meaning already expressed literally by an adjacent word ("filter cigarettes" or "filters");

Finally, several other distinctions, each multiplying the others, give eighty kinds of representation; I only wished to give a small

131

example here of this kind of analysis, which Hindu linguists have pursued to an extremely subtle point.

These two kinds of meaning can suffice in ordinary language. The logicians of the *Nyāya* school maintain that a third function is necessary: *the intention of the statement (tātparya)* which, after the fact, would establish and make known the connection between the meanings of words. But our author, who follows the doctrine of the *Vedānta*, notes that this function is not distinct from the very fact of speaking: it is included in the definition of the sentence. We see here the opposition between the abstract (and here, "realistic") formalism of the *Nyāya* and the active observation of psychological facts which is one of the methods of the *Vedānta*.

3. *The suggestive meaning.* —A transposition by negation made us pass from the literal sense to the figurative sense; in most cases, this would be the same as replacing a *sign-word* with an *image-word.* For practical necessity, it more or less comes down to the same thing as using a literal form *l*: "he's a slanderer" or a figurative form *f*: "he's a viper." The aim of ordinary language, its "fruit" *(phala)*, is in this case to give information about a fact. But in themselves, the propositions *l* and *f* are not equivalent. Everyone feels there is something more in the second than in the first: $f = l + x$; this x, the "surplus of meaning," is what we call the "suggested meaning." And language, inasmuch as it suggests, is said to carry out the function of "suggestion" *(vyanjaña)* or "resonance" *(dhvani)*.

The x of our equation can represent various kinds of suggestion. In "the frock coats entered," this x, combined with other suggestions, could, for example, serve to give me the comic tone I need for my composition. Or else, a figure of rhetoric will be suggested, as in the comparison of the slanderer with a viper. Such suggestions are already encountered in ordinary language. But if we notice that the suggested x is generally, in the final account, the *motive* the speaker had for using *f* instead of *l*, we see that the suggested meaning makes us penetrate the speaker's very thought; we share with him the intention that made him say *f* and not *l*. And in this sharing there is already a rudiment of poetic language. But in ordinary language, the suggested is only an accessory of the literal: it merely attracts attention to the latter or reinforces it. If, on the other hand, the suggested is taken as the principle meaning, then the "fruit" of speech, instead of being simple information, will be a complicity between speaker and listener—and, playing on these complicities, the speaker will be able to use them to lead the listener to the moment of consciousness which is the highest aim of Poetry. In summary, we could say: prose *speaks about* something, poetry *does* something with words.

Thus, they reserve the name resonance *(dhvani)* more specially for the form of signification "in which the suggested, taking precedence over the literal, provokes supernatural Admiration; the term resonance indicates that something resounds within [the discourse]" *(S.D.)*. It is like another dimension of language which, instead of trying to inform (as does a narrative or science) or to guide external action (as does a command), is oriented toward "Savor"—as we have seen it defined above.

> Among other distinctions, "the suggested meaning is different from the literal meaning [as well as from the figurative meaning]:
> "insofar as the *listener (boddhr,* the "perceiver") is concerned, for the literal sense can be perceived by the grammarian, whereas the suggested will be perceived only by the man of sensibility...;
> "insofar as the *means of apprehension* are concerned: the literal is communicated by the utterance of words (the listener being passive), the suggested will only be grasped by the activity of a refined intelligence;
> "insofar as the *effect* is concerned: the literal gives only information *(pratīti),* the suggested will provoke Wonder (thus the gustation of Savor)..." *(S.D.,* V).

I will not get into learned classifications, which finally give a table of 5,355 kinds of suggestion. One of the distinctions we must remember, however, concerns the thing suggested, which can be information about the poem's material subject *(vastu),* a figure of rhetoric, or a Savor. In the first two cases, resonance aims at Savor indirectly, by suggesting its secondary manifestations; in the third case, Savor itself is suggested.

Thus it can happen that Savor is suggested by a literal meaning, with no intermediary other than one of its emotive manifestations. The suggestion is then said to be "of a nonrepresentable course" *(asamlakshyakrama),* for the passage from the literal to the suggested depends not on art, but on human nature. We could find a hundred examples of this in Racine,

SCHEMA OF THE POETIC OPERATION
ACCORDING TO HINDU THEORY
"Gustation of the self's own form"

SAVOR (rasa)
endowed with 3 principle "merits" (guna)

ESSENCE OF THE POEM				ESSENCE OF THE POEM
	SWEETNESS which melts	EVIDENCE which enlightens	ENERGY which enflames	

and distinguished into

Erotic	Furious	Heroic	Horrible
Comic	Pathetic	Marvellous	Terrible
Love	Anger	Heroism	Disgust
Gaiety	Sorrow	Wonder	Terror

DOMINANT SENTIMENTS (Sthāyibhāva)
manifested by the representation of their

POET'S AFFECTIVE STATE

OCCASIONAL CAUSES (vibhāva)
EXTERNAL EFFECTS (anubhāva),
ACCESSORY ACCOMPANIMENTS (vyabhicāribhāva).
(Manifestations of emotions, mental operations and bodily states).

LISTENER'S AFFECTIVE STATE

Manifestation of the "merits" (guna) of Savor by the various
kinds of Stylistic MOVEMENTS (rīti):

Vaidarbhī (analytical order of the sentence, easy sonorities)	Lātī and Pāñchālī (intermediaries. especially aiming for clarity)	Gaudī (synthetic order of the sentence, difficult sonorities)

SENTENCE   COMPOSITION
collections of words composing a meaning.

THE WORD (pada) =

"BODY" OF THE POEM

VOCABLE (Shabda) +	SENSE (artha)	**"BODY" OF THE POEM**
logical functions in power: genus, specific quality, substance, action.	suggested by a literal meaning a figurative meaning, or by specification of the general sense.	
sounds of the voice, distinguished by: timbre, duration, tone (in theater: gesture, emphasis, etc.)	figurative (including or not including the literal meaning; motivated or conventional, etc.)	
	literal, genus, quality, substance, action.	

ORNAMENTS (alamkāra)

of the vocable: alliteration,   of the meaning; simile,
rhyme, etc   metaphor, etc.

FAULTS (dosha)
of the vocable (phonetic, grammatical or lexicological), of the
sentence, of the meaning, of Savor.

such as the line *"Je ne l'ai pas encore embrasse aujourd'hui"* [I have not yet kissed him today], where the Savor *vatsala* (maternal love) is evoked by the direct suggestion of one of the emotions which manifest it *(anishtashaṅkā,* "fear that misfortune will befall" the child). In this light, a good way to understand Hindu theory, after this necessarily arid presentation, would be to reread two or three of Racine's tragedies. We would not find in them a single moment of beauty which could not be analyzed, or at least named, in terms of Hindu poetics.

The "Merits."

All of these words and meanings are only the matter of Poetry. This matter must be formed and arranged by an essence, which is Savor. The essence of Poetry possesses certain "specific activities" *(dharma)* or "merits" *(guna),* by which it manifests itself. "The Merits are to Savor what heroism and the like are to the Soul" *(Dhvani,* and *S.D.,* 604). They are of three kinds:[16]

1. *Sweetness:* this is "a refreshment created by the melting of the spirit...manifest, for example, in the Pathetic..." It corresponds to emotions which, in ordinary life, make us feel "tender." Look closely at the metaphor; it is not very different from that of the Sanskrit to "liquefy."

2. *Energy:* this is "the state of being fired, or an expansion of the mind...manifest, for example, in the Heroic..." It corresponds to the emotions which, in ordinary life, "inflame" us, exalt us, provoke an active response.

3. *Evidence:* "that which, existing in all the Savors, pervades

---

16. The theory of *guna* and *rīti* is far from having this coherence and clarity in all the authors. For the school of *rīti* and (but less clearly) for the *A.P., guna* are also the essences of *rīti;* but their reason for being is not explained and they are treated as specific classes of stylistic ornaments. Elsewhere, the question of their relations is hardly raised, and the definitions are vague.

The names of the three fundamental *guna* are respectively: *mādhurya* (from *madhu,* honey or fermented drink), *ojas* (burst, vigor, energy) and *prasāda* (calm, clarity, grace in the sense of royal or divine grace). The word "spirit" somewhat arbitrarily translates *citta:* the totality (temporarily considered a homogenous matter) of all that, in man, can receive impressions *(vrtti)* and react to these impressions (according to the *Yoga*).

the heart as fire spreads through dry fuel." This comparison, usually applied to thought, to comprehension *(buddhi)*, indicates that this third Merit has as its function to *make something understood*, whereas the two others have as their specific action to *make something felt;* more precisely to make one feel and the other act. That's why Evidence, the direct light of poetic speech (different from the reflected light of the logical discourse), must always be present to illuminate emotions, to make them appear as objects in the light of Savor.

These definitions of the Merits may seem somewhat obscure. We will understand them better by noting that they are constructed on the symbols of water and fire. Sweetness possesses two of water's qualities: freshness and fluidity; Energy, two of fire's qualities: heat and expansivity; Evidence suggests both the limpidity of water and the light of fire.

Sweetness and Energy correspond to two extreme types of emotion, between which all the others fall; and Evidence lights them all. The listener does not passively submit to the emotions evoked by the poet: he makes them his own without making himself theirs. He actively tastes them as an internal spectacle, and it's only through the detachment he feels from his own emotions that the latter can fully blossom, and that Savor can "shine in its own light." A man who wishes only to move other men by his words can be an orator or a sorcerer, but not a poet. The poet, as he stirs a man's feelings, sometimes melting him, sometimes inflaming him, must never stop reminding him: it is not *I* who am moved—just as on the battlefield Krishna reminded Arjuna: "it is not I who act" *(Bhaguvud Gita).*

One or the other of these three functions can be predominant in the poem. Each is manifested in certain syntactic turns of phrase, certain stylistic figures, certain phonetic combinations. We will not give the table of these correspondences which, of course, were only established for the Sanskrit tongue (from which its derivations, the dramatic *prākrits*, were deduced, following precise rules).

Stylistic movements.

Essentially, however, and independently of the language used, the Merits of Savor are manifested in certain types of organization of the poetic matter, which are words, sounds and meanings.

For simplicity's sake, let's take an example from ordinary language. Assume that we were walking together, and in front of me you saw a hole in the ground into which I would fall if I weren't careful. You would warn me with a sentence which would express three things: (a) the fact that there is a hole; (b) the fear I should have of it; (c) the motor reaction which will prevent the accident. Thus you will say, for example: "(a) there's a hole, (b) look out! (c) you're going to fall." But you could also say: "look out! there's a hole; you're going to fall." More generally, you could use one of the six orders *abc, acb, bac, bca, cab, cba*. This choice is not arbitrary; if you try the six possibilities one after the other, you will feel that each one corresponds to a particular attitude of yours and to a particular relation between the elements expressed. This attitude, furthermore, depends on the situation. If I am several steps away from the hole, you could allow yourself to use the quasi-syllogistic order *acb*; but if my foot is already on the edge of the hole, without even thinking you will use order *bca*, in which emotion takes precedence, commanding much quicker action.

The example is quite schematic; but such orders of appearance and connection of meanings are what Hindu rhetoricians call *rīti*, literally: "ways of flowing, speeds, movements." We will call them Stylistic Movements—as we speak of an oratory or musical movement—but we will not translate *rīti* as "style," as is usually done. For us, style is a characteristic of the writer's personality, whereas the Hindu poet must be able to handle all Movements equally well. In this he is an artisan, like the shoemaker who knows how to make mountain-climbing boots and formal pumps; whereas the Western artist, having found the "style" best conforming to his mood, his favorite poses, his habits, his impotence, most often stays with this mannerism, not wishing to change. The first way of seeing, furthermore, has nothing specifically Hindu about it; as in many other matters, it is modern, urban Western civilization that differs from the immense rest of the world. If we ourselves weren't impregnated with this civilization, the preeminence it gives personality in the so-called artist would seem to us, in the totality of human history, a peculiarity hardly worth mentioning.

"An arrangement of words, analogous to the arrangements of parts of the body determined by the attitude of the totality and subordinated to Savor" constitutes each type of Stylistic

Movement (*S.D.*, IX). Sanskrit syntax is highly supple; in particular, it can be more analytical or more synthetic, depending on whether it uses few or many compounds.[17] The length and frequency of these compounds will thus be one of the most externally visible characteristics of each *rīti*. Movements are named after peoples, probably by analogy with the fundamental tendencies of these peoples' speech. They fall between two extremes:

Vaidarbhī, manifesting Sweetness, poor in compounds, thus not requiring the listener to pay close attention from first to last word. The sounds used are easily pronounced, the breath-pauses frequent, the stylistic ornaments uncomplicated. Thus the listener is put into a state of relaxation and prepared to

17. Here, insofar as one can give a translation, is a stanza of benediction intended, at the beginning of a theatrical play, to call the protection of Shiva down on the actors and spectators. The words joined by a hyphen form, in Sanskrit, a single compound word; I have preserved the exact order of the images and one or two alliterations: "On-his-head-the-thunderous-knocking-of-the-tumultuous-swells-of-the-river-of-the-immortals-high-throwing-water-in-dust-disguises-the-violent-spurt-toward-the-swarm-of-stars-by-myriads, [when]-his-foot-hurling-sceptre-standing-swirls-and-furious-cyclone-raises-a-wind-carrying-off-in-a-whirlwind-the-original-eggshell-of-the-world, may it spread His grace, this dance of the Lord-of-Peace, on you!" In this stanza, the Merit called *Energy* predominates.

Here, on the other hand, is a stanza in which the process of composition is hardly used at all, and in which *Sweetness* predominates:

"Not one stream not embellished by the lotus,
not one lotus not fertilized by a bee,
not one bee which didn't buzz softly,
not one buzzing which didn't delight the heart."

(You will perhaps be curious about the meters used. That of the 1st stanza is: − − − − x − −, x x x x x x −, −x− −x− − repeated four times; that of the 2nd: x − x −, − x x − x − x − repeated four times.)

We should not seek in these approximative translations anything other than the opposition I tried to show between two syntactic turns. I leave the reader the pleasure of discovering the two types of Stylistic Movements themselves in Bossuet, who commanded a broad range of them. Whence the distances we hear his voice cross over, and that vast resonance of cathedrals echoing through every sentence of the *Funeral Orations*.

taste emotions of the "melting" sort.

Gaudī, manifesting Energy. The long and numerous compounds require sustained attention; the consonant combinations call for a continuous muscular tension in the vocal apparatus, and long sequences must be spoken in a single breath. Thus the listener is physiologically and psychologically held under pressure and prepared for the emotions that call for an energetic internal response.

Two intermediate Movements (or one, or three, or four, according to other authors) are described, the analysis of which would be less useful. Let us note that the Merit called Evidence has no corresponding Movement of its own; in all types of composition, it must be manifested by "words that evoke their meanings as soon as they are heard."

The "Ornaments."

"The Ornaments *(alamkāra)* are to the language of Poetry what bracelets, earrings, etc., are to the human figure... Their function is to raise Poetry, and they are in the service of Savor" *(S.D.,* I, 3, 5; X, 631). Thus, they are not essential to Poetry and, although Poetry without any ornamentation at all is scarcely conceivable, they do not have the primary role that certain authors ascribe to them. Some of these ornaments correspond closely enough to our "rhetorical figures" for us to suppose they have Greek origins.[18] This assumption is neither proven

18. A large development in dramatic literature and in intentionally ornamental poetry, contrasting with the simplicity of the ancient epic style, was pursued from the 2nd to the 4th centuries of our age (3rd century, Gupta dynasty) — an epoch of intense and fertile exchanges between the Greek and Hindu cultures. These were deliberate exchanges rather than enforced influences: while borrowing the terminology and certain methods of calculation from the Greeks, Hindu astronomy remained quite Hindu. Someone will raise the example of the "Greco-Buddhistic" sculptress, who represents an unfortunate case of crossbreeding. But it's precisely because the sculptress of Gandhara was a Buddhist, and not properly Hindu, that she could degenerate so easily into foreign contamination. The Greek contribution could not, in that case, be grafted into a vigorous tradition, since the characteristic of Buddhism in India was to break with tradition (often scorned by the new religion), particularly in the area of the arts. An art with Buddhic subjects has, it is true, produced marvels (statues, bas-reliefs, temples, frescoes); but it jointly used Hindu subjects (Buddha taking his place among the manifestations of Vishnu, after

nor unlikely. But the manner in which the ornaments are analyzed is typically Hindu, the value of each figure residing in the poet's intention, in the motivation he could have to use it "to serve Savor": the same combinations of sounds, for example, could be a fault or an ornament, depending on whether it is accidental or intentional.

The ornaments fall into one of two categories:

1. *Ornaments of sound:* those which would disappear if one replaced the words conveying them by other, synonymous words (thus the *S.D.* correctly includes the "compound ornaments"—involving both sound and meaning—described by certain authors). The major ones are *alliteration, rhyme, plays on words* and *double meanings* (double meaning of the vocable which must, let's not forget, be resolved in a single meaning of the word; otherwise it would be "ambiguity," which is a fault). As a reminder the author cites an inferior form of amusement: the arrangement of letters whose graphic transcription reproduces the drawing "of a lotus, a saber, a drum, a wheel, a stream of cow's urine," etc.—ornaments always being for the ear, nonetheless. The ornaments of sound must be subject to the laws of correspondence between phenomena and savors.

2. *Ornaments of meaning or sense:* the *S.D.* describes 79 of them, of which several possess numerous varieties, sub-varieties, modalities, etc. The analysis of these ornaments is often quite subtle and conforms to the general laws of signification: an *alamkāra* is not used in a haphazard way, but responds to a particular psychological operation, a certain attitude and distance that the speaker takes with respect to language. Most of the ornaments of meaning are varieties of explicit or implicit comparison *(upamā)*. *Metaphor (rūpaka), contrast*, the various kinds of *synecdoche, paradox,* etc., are represented with numerous modalities.

Only one of these 79 ornaments, the 68th, which is treated in several words, contains what for us has become an entire

Rāma and Krishna, just as with the Muslims Christ takes his place among the Prophets): insofar as it was traditional, it was Hindu—not Buddhistic—art.

literary school: the "description of Nature" *(svabhāvokti)*. Thus, one of our great aesthetic provinces, the imitation of Nature, is reduced by the Hindus to a small, infrequently used ornament which it would be in bad taste to abuse. Moreover, this ornament is restricted to "the description of an object's appearance or specific action, which is difficult to perceive"; it should never to taken by the poet as an end in itself.

It would be easy (but I would never finish) to illustrate, by analyzing ornaments of meaning, the theory that I initially posited about the passage from one degree of signification to another using a particular sign. Each of these ornaments is actually a sign that alerts the listener to the fact that the object spoken of belongs to an order of representation other than that of natural objects; just as in theater, a given adornment, diadem or facial painting tells us that the actor represents a given hero or god.

The faults.

"The faults *(dosha)* such as cacophony, incomplete meaning, etc., depreciate Savor through sounds and meanings, as the fact of being one-eyed, lame, etc., depreciates a person through his body. Faults such as using the technical term for a manifestation [when one wishes to provoke it] directly depreciate Savor which is the essence of the poem, as stupidity, for example, depreciates the person in his very essence" *(S.D.,* I).

This latter sort of fault is thus the most serious. We could call it "prosaism," since it consists of speaking about something instead of making something *be.* We are given as example: "she felt shame." This phrase only gives us information; they should have said, poetically, something like: "she lowered her eyes...," in order to lead the listener to recreate in himself the precise emotion which, in the given situation, could provoke this bodily manifestation.

These faults are called *faults of Savor.* The others are of three kinds:

1. *Faults of the vocable* (which can be eradicated by the appropriate substitution of a single word); they can be phonetic *("Et son carquois oisif à son côté pendait")*; grammatical (solecism, barbarism); semantic (improper use, uselessness, etc.); or lexicological (unjustified archaism, obsolete word, etc.).

2. *Faults of the sentence:* mistakes in syntax, useless redundancy, involuntary pun, etc.; faults of prosody are also included in this category.

3. *Faults of meaning:* contradictions between literal and suggested meanings, improper order of images, useless repetition, opposition to scientific truth, etc.

In certain cases, some faults stop being faults: for example, cacophony and obscurity when a grammarian is supposedly speaking (the almost algebraic terminology of Hindu linguistics is often quasi-unpronounceable). Some faults even become ornaments in specific cases. Thus the "opposition to recognized facts" becomes an ornament in the case of accepted "poetic conventions."

> (These are some of the conventions: "The sky and sin are depicted as being black; fame and gaiety as white; anger and passion, red; one describes lotus plants and water lilies growing even in rivers and the sea;...the Tchakora bird drinks moonbeams...the Ashoka tree flowers when a woman kicks it...Love's arrows pierce the hearts of the young, and they say the same thing about women's glances...peacocks dance at the rumbling of thunder...[etc.] Many other poetic conventions can be found in the words of true poets."[19]

19. It seems to me that here, as elsewhere at times, the work of Jean Paulhan *(Les Fleurs de Tarbes)* encounters the observations of Hindu rhetoricians. The latter have, in particular, examined the causes of these impressions of bad taste, verbosity, etc., which stereotyped stylistic figures can produce in us. These causes are, among others: the "dubious preeminence" granted to the literal, figurative or suggested meanings; the "equal preeminence" of the suggested and the literal; the "incomplete blossoming" of the meaning aimed at by the poet; etc. In short, the unpleasant impression would come from the fact that we hesitate to interpret the word as a sign-word or an image-word, and our reprobation goes toward the author who has let himself be carried away by the mechanisms of language, carrying us off with him. One easily accepts words such as "achieve, decide, step," which are essentially extremely stereotyped metaphors, because the metaphors they dissimulate ([bring] to a head, cut off, staff or rod) have been forgotten in favor of a simple conventional meaning. We accept "to pardon the years' inexcusable insult" because the literal contradiction must necessarily be resolved in a figure which will be understood as such (*virodha,* "contradiction"); or again, "by what love you were wounded," because what follows, "and died...," restores all the image's force and reassures us as to the intention of the poet—who, by a skillful feint,

The degrees of Poetry.

Up to this point, we have spoken almost exclusively of the highest kind of Poetry, that which is "animated by Savor" and which aims at producing "gustation" by means of "Resonance." Thus one groups among the superior forms of Poetry those in which gustation of the essence yields (at least momentarily) to the awakening, in the listener, of the manifestations of this essence. The poet will bring a certain sentiment to life in the listener, without representing the object of this sentiment to him. And since, as we have said, the listener remains a spectator of his own emotions — all the while tasting this sentiment — he will feel that something is lacking from this representation: the essential meaning of the poem will, in some way, be suggested by its very absence as an unattained object. For example, the so-called "Erotic" Savor is only fully evoked in the case of a mutual love between a man and a woman of superior natures. A love directed toward a being higher than ordinary humanity — god, sage, spiritual master — cannot be fully "tasted." We have only a feeling of it, not knowledge; and Savor is knowledge. This is what we call *savor-sentiment*. Inversely, a love which is not mutual, or between inferior persons or animals, is but an analogy of love. This is what we call *reflected sentiment*. An emotion attributed to an improper subject, such as modesty to a prostitute, constitutes a *reflected sentiment*. Finally, a sentiment can be evoked as *nascent*, as *dying*, or as *combined* or *mixed* with another sentiment. In all of these cases, a somewhat complex sentiment is aroused in the listener without his hav-

made us doubt his vigilance and freedom for a moment. But phrases such as "the insult of the years" or "the wounds of passion" would leave us indecisive and unsatisfied. The poor use of ornaments also coincides with the "non-dissimulation" of the technical process, where we see the ornament used without any true necessity, simply out of a desire to create an effect (*S.D.*, IV, concerning poetry of the inferior kind in which Resonance is subordinated) [slightly revised note].

ing the full knowledge that would be the "gustation of Savor."
Nonetheless, this is still a poetic operation—less perfect, but
not worthless (*S.D.*, IV).

On the other hand, if "resonance" is not the principal meaning of the poem (either because the technical procedures are
too visible, or because there is doubt about the true meaning),
we are dealing with poetry of an inferior kind. Some authors
classify compositions from which all resonance is absent (pure
description, virtuosity, etc.) as being even lower. The school
we are following says, "This is not poetry at all" (*S.D.*, IV).

Poetic forms.

No doubt you have already been surprised to hear me speak
at such length about the poetic art without saying one word
about metrics. This is because metrics and poetry are completely
independent of each other for the Hindus. Their most arid, most
abstract treatises are almost always written in verse, for
mnemonic reasons. Thanks to this, some very old texts have
been transmitted without alteration all the way to the present.
Their corruption usually begins as soon as they are written down
and carelessly distributed in the form of books. A great number
of somewhat complicated meters, however, are usually not used
in didactic works, but rather are reserved for poetry. Since
nothing escapes the Hindus' analogical and classifying mentality, each meter has been attributed a specific divinity, meaning and usage. Correspondences have been established between
Savors and meters: it is clear that rapid and bouncing succes-
sions of short syllables would not be appropriate for conveying
melancholy, and that heavy, dragging series of long syllables
would go badly with war-like agitation, etc. (*N.S.*, XVII, 99ff.).[20]

The poem can also be in "prose," whether free or "with metric
flavor" (rhythmic prose); or again, verse and prose mixed (I use

20. Classical versification comprises:

1) A single kind of verse *with a fixed number of syllables and partially
fixed quantity:* the epic *shloka*, a vestige of Vedic metrics. More than
three-fourths of classical literature, whether stories, epics, technical
or scientific treatises (as mnemonic verse), etc., is written in this meter,
which is much more common than prose. It is used in stanzas of 4
lines, each with 8 syllables, the odd lines required not to end and the
two evens to end with two iambs.

2) A great variety of meters with *a fixed number of syllables and
quantities:* about twenty of these meters are common (from 11 x 4 to

the term "prose" here to mean "non-metrical").

I understand: you are astonished because the word "rhythm" has not yet been pronounced. The Hindus have never had the ludicrous idea, which we have in the West, of confusing "rhythm" and "meter." If you do not get too attached to words, you will remember that in this study rhythm was described as an essential characteristic of the "body of poetry." Rhythm is in fact inseparable from what we have called "stylistic movements." These "movements," with their endless varieties, are defined, as we have seen, as the simultaneous arrangements of sounds and meanings, determined by the speaker's attitude—as in the bodily analogy. Since the body of the poem is composed of *sounds* (provided by the voice), *images* (provided by the literal meanings which subsist under figurative meanings), *concepts* (figurative meanings) and *emotions* (suggested), rhythm must result from the balance and composition of these various elements in action. Meter properly speaking is only the "envelope" (*chandas*) or the "form" (*vrtti*) given to the general movement of poetic matter. Poetry is not unilinear: it is an art of simultaneities, in which matters subject to radically different laws (sounds of the voice, images, concepts, emotions) must be arranged by the poet's will with a common goal in mind. It is in this sense that Poetry was created based on the analogy of life, the poem created in man's image. This is what Hindu poetics can teach us that is useful.

When the poet in full possession of the science of speech unites sound and sense, he simultaneously brings about

21 x 4 syllables; v. note 17).

3) A type of meter with *fixed quantity and variable number of syllables*, analogous to Greco-Latin meters. The most common is the *āryå*, which is measured thus (each number represents a foot and gives its duration in short syllables): 4, 4, 4 − 4, 4, 4, 4, 1 − 4, 4, 4 − 4, 4, 1, 4, 1; the amphibrach proscribes unstressed feet, and the endings of lines 2 and 4 are left to the poet's discretion.

The poetic genres, characterized by their external presentation (length, use of verse or prose, etc.), are so numerous, so supple, so able to be mixed and modified, that their rules and classifications practically equal total freedom: not the freedom of whim, but freedom for the poet to choose the most appropriate external discipline.

this union in himself; thus he is all-powerful over himself. "A single word," it is said, "if it is well used and perfectly understood, is the Cow from which we draw all desires in this world and in the heavens." But "the man who wishes to utter a word before an audience without having studied the science of speech, is like he who wishes to capture an elephant in heat with a lotus leaf."

Would knowing this theory enable us to apply it? Far from it. For, first of all, the frequent reference to bodily analogy links poetry tightly with dance. It lets us suppose, behind the theory, a practical and direct teaching which no book can convey. Next, to create poetry is to wish to reach its final goal: a goal that is both higher than those ever ascribed to it in the West, and that nonetheless remains relative, since Poetry is a means of helping our deficient reason attain the unveiled teaching of truth. Finally, to be a poet presupposes that one has already taken several steps on the path of this teaching, since the poet's task is to draw us toward it "by offering us a sweet, a savor to be tasted," by creating an intimate complicity between us and himself, by leading us to the moment of a little more lucidity, which he will take advantage of in order to plant a word in us — a word which could not have germinated otherwise.

Do such poets exist? Certainly, the Earth has borne some. And if the classical poets of post-Buddhic India are not such poets — no more than ours — it is nonetheless this idea of the poet that guided and fertilized the efforts of the best among them. Long and severe efforts, as it is said in the *Agni Purāna:* "In this world, it is difficult to reach manhood; and from there, very difficult to attain knowledge; from there, it is difficult to reach the status of poet; and from there, very difficult to attain creative power."

(1937.)

SOME FRENCH POETS OF THE 25TH CENTURY

We have chosen these excerpts from a future anthology from among the texts most accessible to a 20th-century reader – and from among the most "human," in the meaning (if it is a meaning) we give this word: that is, neither the best nor the worst. The necessity of translation posed some very delicate problems for us. Despite all the fears, in the 20th century, that advertising, newspapers, radio and technical jargon could make people "conceive of" (as they strangely used to say), French in the 25th century maintained the privilege of being a language in which nothing vague could be correctly stated. At the same time, thanks to judicious borrowings from various other languages, it recovered the richness and substantiality of images which the 16th century's rigorous surgery had deprived it of. In other respects, what a change! Closely following the fate of Anglo-American, French became a kind of Chinese, a quasi-monosyllabic language, whose constituent elements were stereotyped phrases, held together by relations of tonic accent and order of sequence. Our translations, alas, often "sacrifice" – let us note here that in the 20th century, "sacrifice" implies "to lose" and "to diminish" – often "sacrifice," we were saying, in the intellectual sense, the poems' "incantatory"[1] value. "We beg the pardon" – as they said in the 20th century, when, in fact, they were quite prone to begging pardon for anything, forgetting that they were part of the hierarchy implied in the notion of pardon – "of our dear readers," according to the consecrated

---

1. This word translates the verb *san-sing-tu:* "to lead by means of a song." For example, the "neo-birds" produced by chromosomatic grafts, which in the 25th century replace the ancient "passenger airplanes," are *san-sing-tuized* to serve as a means of locomotion for man; the "neo-cows," all udder, produced by new methods of tissue cultivation, are *san-sing-tuized* to provide man with nutritious and good-tasting milk; etc.

magic formula, whose power was still so great at that time that the thus-honored readers naively assumed the right to pardon, everyone then being convinced that this difficult operation of pardoning was indeed accomplished. In certain cases, however, we have only been able to keep the approximate flavor of certain expressions by adopting compromises between the two languages.

To give some "idea" of the difficulties involved in being understood from one era to another, let us recall that around the year 2440 everyone called it a joke and a paradox when Professor Snifl proclaimed that in the 19th and 20th centuries, no one even suspected that poetry should and must be founded on an experienced knowledge of man and language – that the poets of the time did not feel obliged to undergo any apprenticeship of the "internal trade"; that there was no poetic teaching; that poetry was generally considered the combination of a mysterious "gift" and a certain external know-how; and that one could very well be called a "poet" while being a confused intellectual, a drunkard, a chatterer or an ambitious person. Nonetheless, Snifl rested his case on period documents, before which his opponents were forced to concede. It is also true that in the 25th century, if poets claimed to work according to an internal science and technique of utterance and meaning, this was often only a claim; there was, for the most part, a chasm between theory and fact – as you will be able to guess from the several examples which follow.

Careful, as we have said, to present works easily accessible to 20th-century readers, we will choose our excerpts principally from among the "writists"–somewhat archaic poets, who transmitted their work by means of a written language, using photographic reproduction, microfilm, or even ancient typographical processes.

Roger Notorious (2330-2431) is this group's dominant figure. He is especially famous for his research into the "curvature of the number system," and the three tercets he placed at the head of his treatise on this subject are one of the finest examples of "mathematical lyricism" so popular at the time. Here is the translation:

After space and time
Numbers must also be curved,
The way one lays down to die.

There is an absolute number
After which one can no longer count,
As one can no longer count on oneself.

On oneself and not on one's fingers,
When one lays down to die,
On oneself, but who is counting?

His *Perfunctory Biography Dictated by the Author on His Deathbed* is also worth quoting in its entirety:

I was born without knowing a word,
at the age of fifteen I knew ten thousand,
and was no better off.

At twenty I knew a hundred thousand,
but I understood nothing
except screams.

At thirty I learned to howl
when I felt myself cut
in two but always whole.

At forty,
thanks to the patience of my masters,
I learned to say a few words.

At sixty I surrounded myself
with a wall of speech
to protect my silence.

At eighty,
to my eighty grandchildren,
I told six hundred forty thousand stories.

At one hundred I packed my bags,
put the key under the mat
and said, "Good night, everyone."

Jean Dussucre (2345-2429), a student and collaborator of Roger Notorious, was also a very effective poet. Appointed Census Expert to the Ethical Congress of Timbuktu in 2400, he satirized the attending Heads of State in an improvised quatrain that resolved a difficult international tension in gales of laughter. We shall quote this quatrain, with the indispensable commentaries:

QUATRAIN IMRPOVISED AT THE
ETHICAL CONGRESS OF TIMBUKTU IN
THE YEAR 2400

You are all so intelligent,[2]
you are all so good-hearted,[3]
and you are all so tough,[4]
that you all take your hats off to each other.[5]

In an altogether different vein is the work of *Agreeable Auguste* (2380-2445), the great subterranean traveler, who was condemned to death and autolysized during the dictatorship of the Counterthingamajigs for having owned an electric razor. His poems, songs, epigrams, fables and anecdotes were very popular in all social strata. He enriched the language with numerous sayings, proverbs and metaphors. Here are two of his short poems:

VERBIAGE

I same, I have always samed and I always will same, with all my samity. Liker I can't, otherer I won't, samer I am. And by mumbo!

2. Allusion, no doubt, to the Protarch of Chtibya, who had just published his *Epistemology with Multiple Reference-Points*, in which he proved that two and two were four *more so* for a sated man than for a starving one.

3. Probably addressed to Nervusrex, sovereign of all the villages in Australia with a population of less than 800, who had successfully performed the first animal-vegetable graft. By intergrafting the chromosomes of a lettuce and a wild rabbit, he had hoped to put an end to the age-old conflicts between sedentaries and nomads: the sedentaries would hunt salad and the nomads would plant rabbits. We know the experiment's lamentable results: everything mineralized.

4. This line was aimed at the "Ingenious Republicans," who had so perfected tissue cultivation that the expression "cannon fodder" [*chair à canon: literally, "canon flesh"—Trans.*] ceased to be a simple metaphor.

5. Play on words untranslatable in the 20th century. "Hat" translates *tyos-tyat*, a kind of visored cap: the word already seems to have appeared in Parisian lingo around 1940.

Let us same, samers, with all our samity.

You say this hurts me? If it adorns, it's all the same to me, and by mumbo or by jumbo, I same myself and I same you back, false samers, with all my samity.

I'll bet you ten thousand perhapses against a sack full of supposings that despite all your samity, you could not same my same, and by mumbo or by jumbo, by hogwash or brainwash, I will same always and everywhere, abundantly.

THE PAWN, THE POST AND THE LYRIPIPED,
a fable.

A pawn was pawnsive: "I am low on lyricism,
I have a good head on my shoulders, but no wing on
*   my feet.*
Why can't I poster, why can't I pedal, why can't I
*   lyripipawn!"*
Now, a post passing by with big booms of the bass
*   drumstick*
heard this gloom and said between two yawns:
"Don't be so pawnsive, you look like a poet
*   but rather send your foot*
*   into the rear of my drumsticker."*

The pawn took this sound advice
and was immediately impounded:
now he's only a lyripiped.

Another enemy of neo-mechanism, *Julius Plaster,* wrote *Jeremiads in the Old Style,* like this:

Get thee gone, wicked crows,[6]
*   from 'neath my feet;*
let me tend to that which grows
*   of earth and peat,*

leading the poets who used them to sell their services to rich breeders, and certainly harming the purity of their intentions.

Reacting against these tendencies, the *New Bards,* desirous of restoring to poetry its direct effectiveness, traveled through-

---

6. He is speaking here, of course, of the "neo-crows" of cultivation, used by the garbage-collection service.

out the country in small groups, singing, dancing, miming, chronicling, mocking, amusing and edifying. No written document has survived which would allow us to give a sample of their poetry, except for four lines of an invective aimed by a group of New Bards at the members of a famous learned society, who took the former to court, causing these lines to be recorded in the trial evidence:

> Curved slugs, pompous caterpillars, philosophizing,
> wriggling about, capped fatheads, happy mugs,
> already rotten, but full of hope,
> already putrid, covered with honors...

A similar desire for effectiveness gave birth to "intrusionist poetry." The *Intrusionists* considered poetry to be a powerful psychological lever. According to them, a poem must change the reader in a real and lasting way. The intrusionist poem, generally very short and written in very simple language, is characterized by the fact that it is accompanied by "instructions for use," brief stage directions indicating the conditions under which the reader must "take" the poem. "Otherwise," says the poetess *Compelline Trare* (2500-2585), the school's founder, "it's as if you had medicines without knowing how to swallow them, that you merely looked at... Eat! I give you the drug and the way to use it." Here, among many possible examples, is a short intrusionist poem by *Joliboaboa* (2509-2545):

THE INVISIBLE MAN

(To be recited at night before going to bed, in front of a mirror; naked with a hat on your head, plugging your ears with your thumbs, fingers spread. Learn the poem by heart,[7] then recite it once looking yourself straight in the eyes, and a second time with eyes closed, beginning with the last line.)

> I spent my day very intelligently,
> And night comes, bearing its reward.
> I showed my facade, no one saw my face;
> I saw nothing, and no one saw me.
> I would say, "I am the invisible man,"
> If I really were sure of being a man.

7. It is difficult to know if the expression we translate as "by heart" indeed means, as in the 25th century, "by means of the heart," or if it has the meaning "by head" that it usually does in the 20th century.

The last intrusionist poems—those of the final twenty years of the century—unfortunately lapsed into low-brow sorcery.

Already in the 22nd century, various groups of poets, seeking a truly universal language, had tried to express themselves by means of ideograms. Their rather disappointing attempts yielded works which were at times childish, at times recondite—and often both at once. In the period that interests us, the *Ideographists* were almost exclusively humorists or parlor poets. Several of them produced charming opuscules; but as we are only concerned with French-language poets, we will leave them aside.

Let us simply quote the poetess *Esbigne Ova* (2431-2500), who, after having produced ideographist poems that reflected some of the period's mystical preoccupations, returned to vocal poetry. Here is an example of her later work, the translation of which gave us no end of headaches:

GRAVELY

Remirror from the depth of lyre, along the writings,
none one that is the question
of worst wolf.
Never never a retort
tit for tat
which gashes—
what slashes—
the lair
lair is here, lair is there,
lair weighs, lair pays,
lair gives me a bone
and two and three and all.

The wear,
wear is here, wear is there,
wear teases, wear pleases,
wear gives me a bone
and two and three and all.

The air,
air is here, air is there,
air chimes, air peels,
the air, the wear, the lair.

But the lair of the worst wolf
slashing the retort
hones me to the wind—where are you going?

And yet we will pull through
by packing the final trunk
as long as light strikes
in the depths.

But where is the poetry in all this, you ask? True poetry, great poetry, the kind that lifts you up, hair on end and throat dry, that splits you like a diamond in your component parts, and simultaneously puts you back together like a straight arrow shot off at a speed at which everything dies in light—poetry which grips, guides, inflames and destines, true poetry, great poetry?

That poetry is not future, it is not past, it is or it is not. When one speaks about it, it is not. In the silence beyond time where poetry keeps watch, let us plunge without a thought of return. Many will drown there; a few will make poetry gush forth.

(1940-41.)

POETRY BLACK, POETRY WHITE

As with magic, poetry is black or white, depending on whether it serves the sub-human or the superhuman.

The same innate tendencies govern the machinery of the white poet and the black poet. Some call these tendencies a mysterious gift, a mark of superior powers; others an infirmity or a curse. No matter. Or rather, yes! – it matters highly, but we have not yet reached the point of being able to understand the origin of our essential structures. He who could understand them would deliver himself from them. The white poet seems to understand his poetic nature, to free himself from it and make it serve. The black poet uses it and becomes its slave.

But what is this "gift" common to all poets? It is a particular connection between the various lives which make up our life, such that each manifestation of one of them is no longer simply its exclusive sign, but could become, through an internal resonance, a sign of the emotion that at a given moment is one's own color, sound or taste. This central emotion, deeply hidden within us, vibrates and shines only in rare instants. For the poet, these instants will be poetic moments, and at such a moment all his thoughts, feelings, movements and words will be the signs of this central emotion. And when the unity of their meaning is realized in an image stated in words, then most especially will we say that he is a poet. This is what we will call the "poetic gift," for want of knowing more about it.

The poet has a rather unclear notion of his gift. The black poet exploits it for his personal satisfaction. He believes that he can take credit for this gift, that he himself voluntarily makes poems. Or else, giving in to the mechanism of resonant meanings, he prides himself on being possessed by a superior mind, which has chosen him as its medium. In both cases, the poetic gift serves only pride and delusive imagination. Whether schemer or visionary, the black poet lies to himself and believes he is someone. Pride, lies – still a third term characterizes him:

laziness. Not that he doesn't act and struggle, or that it seems to come from outside. But all this movement happens by itself; he keeps from personally intervening *himself*—this poor, naked self that wants neither to be seen nor to see itself as poor and naked, that each of us tries so hard to conceal under masks. It is the "gift" that operates in him, and he takes pleasure in it, like a voyeur, without showing himself. He wraps himself in it the way the soft-bellied hermit crab takes shelter and adorns itself in the shell of the murex, made to produce royal purple and not to clothe shameful little runts. Laziness at seeing oneself, at being seen; fear of having no richness other than the responsibilities one assumes: this is the laziness I'm speaking of—oh mother of all my vices!

Black poetry is fertile in wonders like dreams and opium. The black poet tastes every pleasure, adorns himself in every ornament, exercises every power—in his imagination. The white poet prefers reality, even paltry reality, to these rich lies. His work is an incessant struggle against pride, imagination and laziness. Accepting his gift, even if he suffers from it and suffers from suffering, he seeks to make it serve ends greater than his selfish desires: the as-yet-unknown cause of this gift.

I will not say: so-and-so is a white poet, so-and-so is a black poet. This would be to fall from ideas into opinions, discussions and error. I will not even say: so-and-so has the poetic gift, so-and-so does not. Do I have it? Often I doubt it; sometimes I strongly believe I do. I am never certain once and for all. Each time dawn appears, the mystery is there in its entirety. But if I was once a poet, I wish to be a white one. In fact, all human poetry is a mixture of white and black; but some tends toward whiteness, the other blackness.

That which tends toward blackness need make no effort. It follows the natural, sub-human downward slope. One need not make an effort to brag, to dream, to lie and be lazy; nor to calculate and scheme, when calculating and scheming are for the benefit of vanity, imagination or inertia. But white poetry goes uphill. It swims upstream like the trout to go spawn in its birthplace. It holds fast, by force and by cunning, against the whims of the rapids and the eddies. It does not let itself be distracted by the shimmering of passing bubbles, nor be swept away by the current toward soft, muddy valleys.

How does the poet who wants to become white wage this battle? I will tell you how I try to wage it, in my rare better moments, so that one day, if I am a poet, my poetry—grey as it may be—will exude at least a desire for whiteness.

I will distinguish three phases of the poetic operation: the luminous seed, the clothing in images, and verbal expression.

Every poem is born of a seed, dark at first, which we must make luminous for it to produce fruits of light. With the black poet, the seed remains dark and produces blind, subterranean vegetation. To make it shine, one must create silence, for this seed is the Thing-to-be-said itself, the central emotion that seeks to express itself through my whole machine. The machine by itself is dark, but it likes to proclaim itself luminous, and manages to make itself believed. As soon as it is set in motion by the seed's germination, it claims to be acting under its own steam, it shows off for the perverse pleasure of each of its levers and gears. So be quiet, machine! Work and shut up! Silence to word games, memorized lines, memories fortuitously assembled; silence to ambition, to the desire to shine—for only light shines by itself; silence to self-flattery and self-pity; silence to the rooster who thinks he makes the sun rise! And silence parts the shadows, the seed begins to glow, lighting, not lit. *That* is what you have to do. It is very difficult, but each little effort receives a little glimmer of light in reward. The Thing-to-be-said then appears in its most intimate form, as an eternal certainty—a pinpoint of light containing the immensity of the desire for Being.

The second phase is the clothing of the luminous seed, which reveals but is not revealed, invisible like light and silent like sound—its clothing in the images that will make it manifest. Here again, reviewing these images, one must reject and chain down those which would serve only easiness, lies and pride. So many beauties we would like to show off. But once the order is established, we must let the seed itself choose the plant or animal in which it will clothe itself by giving it life.

And third comes the verbal expression, for which it is no longer a matter simply of internal work, but also of external science and know-how. The seed has its own respiration. Its breath takes possession of the expressive mechanisms by communicating its rhythm to them. Thus, these mechanisms should, first of all, be well oiled and just relaxed enough so that they do not start dancing their own dances and scanning incongruous meters. And as it bends the sounds of language to its breath, the Thing-to-be-said also compels them to contain its images. Now, how does it carry out this double operation? That is the mystery. It is not by intellectual scheming: that would require too much time; nor by instinct, for instinct does not invent. This power is exercised thanks to the particular relation that exists between the various elements of the poet's machinery, and that unites matters as different as emotions, images, concepts and sounds in a single living substance. The life of this new organism is the poet's rhythm.

The black poet does almost precisely the opposite, although the exact semblance of these operations is performed in him. His poetry, of course, opens a number of worlds to him, but they are worlds without Sun, lit by a hundred fantastic moons, populated by phantoms, decorated with mirages and sometimes paved with good intentions. White poetry opens the door to only one world, that of the unique Sun, without false wonders, real.

I have said what one must do to become a white poet. As if it were that easy! Even in prose, in ordinary speech and writing (as in all aspects of my daily life), all that I produce is grey, salt-and-pepper, soiled, a mixture of light and darkness. And so I take up the struggle after the fact. I re-read myself. In my sentences, I see words, expressions, interferences that do not serve the Thing-to-be-said: an image that meant to be strange, a pun that thought it was funny, the pedantry of a certain prig who would do better to stay seated at his desk instead of coming to play the fipple flute in my string quartet. And remarkably enough, it is simultaneously a mistake in taste, style, or even syntax. Language itself seems set up in such a way as to detect the intruders for me. Few mistakes are purely technical. Almost all of them are my mistakes. And I cross out, and I correct, with the joy one can have at cutting a gangrenous limb from one's body.

(1941.)

THE MESSAGE OF THE *BHAGAVAD GITA*[1]

Commentary on sacred texts is one of the modes of literary expression favored by the Hindu masters who wrote in far-distant or recent times. The *Essays on the Gita* by the master of Pondicherry is a work of this kind. One of Sri Aurobindo's earliest disciples, Anilbaran Roy, has put out an abridged edition of these essays (published in Calcutta in 1928), culling from the master's works the English translations of verses from the *Gita*, followed by their respective commentaries. Through this selection and arrangement, the work is made more accessible to the Western reader, who has not been nourished from childhood—as the Hindu has—on this gospel announced in mid-battlefield by Krishna, God made man. The French version of the *Lord's Song*, which faithfully follows the English text compiled by Anilbaran Roy, does not aspire to be more beautiful or more literal than the numerous translations of the sacred poem currently available. Often, in fact, it is a paraphrase, or already an interpretation of the text. It does not aim at giving literary pleasure, but at communicating to the reader the deep meaning and the practical meaning (one not being understood without the other) of Krishna's ancient and ever-current teaching to he who has questions about his present duty, his final destiny, and his eternal essence.

In this traditional garb, Sri Aurobindo's thought can, from certain angles, seem singularly revolutionary to those accustomed to Vedantic scholasticism or to the purely metaphysical position of a René Guénon, for example. A major idea runs through all of Sri Aurobindo's writings (and frequently appears in Vivekananda's work) which, if misunderstood, could lead

1. As interpreted by Sri Aurobindo. Daumal's comments are based on and concern the French translation by Camille Rao and Jean Herbert, published in 1941 in the series "Les Grands Maîtres Spirituels dans l'Inde contemporain" [translator's revised note].

us to see it as a concept of "progress" quite surprising in a Hindu thinker. But we are dealing here with notions that are, in fact, quite foreign to the modern mind. This idea has several facets, and I would like to underline two of them.

First, there is the notion of successive "syntheses" by which, in the course of time, the single and eternal truth adapts (according to Aurobindo) to historical human necessities, to the specific conditions of mores, cults and knowledge. As these conditions change with time, a moment periodically arrives when the expressions of the immutable truth are no longer adapted to man, no longer understood, and thus no longer effective. A reworking of beliefs, doctrines and mental attitudes becomes necessary; a new interpretation of the original words whose wealth of meaning and virtue is inexhaustible; a new synthesis of the traditional elements tending toward disintegration. Thus, according to Aurobindo, there was in India a Vedic synthesis, an Upanishadic synthesis and, more specifically adapted to the modern world, the synthesis of Tantrism and that of the *Bhagavad Gita*, which is the subject of these "commentaries."

The idea's other facet is more difficult to grasp. Sri Aurobindo indeed seems to admit the historical perfectibility of humanity, analogous to the perfectibility of the individual. We admit this second notion willingly enough: it is the basis of all mysticism, of all asceticism. But from the point of view of eternal Truth and Reality, isn't it just as inconceivable as the first? If, from the absolute point of view, everything is realized once and for all, it is just as absurd to speak of individual progress as it is to speak of progress of the species. But we are not speaking from this "point of view"! From *our* point of view, just as we must work long and hard to truly become what we otherwise are only in abstract possibility, and just as this work can transform the individual to the point of making him a new being, a living species of an order superior to those Nature produces—in the same way, couldn't one think that humanity as a whole contains the seed of a fourth biological reign, a future superhumanity? The answer to this question cannot be a peremptory and definitive yes or no. The correct expression of these ideas is very delicate, and to stick to what Aurobindo says on a given page or in a given chapter would be to risk gross errors in interpretation. Let us recall, nonetheless, that this idea of the perfectibility of human nature, which has no place in the *metaphysical doctrine,* is inherent in *religious thought:* the latter does not contradict the former, but rather serves it and illustrates it like a moving image of the Never-changing, as each day dawn follows night, without this affecting the Sun. This idea is thus as inherent in religious thought (which in its expressions is historical, changeable) as the opposite idea of a "Golden" or "Edenic Age": they are two poles of a single idea projected in human chronology. Messianism, the Heavenly City, celestial Jerusalem in the Judeo-Christian traditions, the final salvation of all beings in the religion of Amida, all of these are figures of the same notion, to which the Hindu theory of time-cycles gives a cosmological base. It is from a *practical* point of view—by this I mean aiming at a real usefulness for the man who bears the seed and the desire for *transformation*—that Aurobindo treats these problems, which he studied in a more general and cosmological manner in his commentary on the *Ishā Upanishad.* It always concerns the persistence of the Immutable in the changeable, that is, the very rhythm of this world in its creation, its preservation and its dissolution. In humanity as in the individual, there is no ascent without descent, and "man's progress" is a degradation of ideas.

One cannot summarize Aurobindo's thought without betrayal when he strives to resolve, or rather to dissolve, the great theological and ethical problems posed in the *Gita.* He even takes great care to avoid laying himself open to the systematic philosophical mind; and a sage will never be too careful in this respect, given that we even see a "Socratic philosophical system" plainly exposed in contemporary textbooks! Theological problems (personal God and Absolute God, relations of the soul to God, identifying union or beatific vision, God and the Cosmos, etc.) and ethical problems (contemplation and action, asceticism and quietism, recompense and *karma,* works and detachment from the fruit of these works, etc.): these two classes of problem are, moreover, complementary, and have no meaning unless considered mutually. If you will allow me to explain this assertion by means of an easily grasped example: the Christian belief in a single life on this earth, at the end of which man will be judged definitively and without appeal, is true if the believer consequently understands that he does not have a second to lose in working toward his perfection; it is false if he concludes that, God knowing all, his fate is predestined and he only has to wait in inertia and carelessness. The Hindu belief in a multiplicity of successive existences is true if it inspires man with the ardent desire to break out, in *this* life, of the chains of *karma* (for if he does not take the first step in his present life, why should he take it in a later one?); it is false if he tells himself: "I've got plenty of time!" These two apparently contradictory beliefs are thus true or false together. This does not mean that man's *ethical life* is the foundation and reality of *ideas:* on the contrary! But it is the ground on which these ideas are tested and made manifest, for us as we are.

I hope you will forgive me if, instead of discussing the contents of this book, I have only given vent to several reflections that reading it inspired in me. For me, and I hope it will be the same for you, these reflections, and the ties they have to the most current and pressing problems of daily life, are proof of the work's value and of the infinite fertility of the source from which it draws.

(1941.)

162

THE DETERMINING MEMORY

The fact cannot be recounted. I have tried many times to tell it, in the nearly eighteen years since it happened. I would like to exhaust my linguistic resources once and for all, and report at least the external and material circumstances surrounding it. This fact, accidentally acquired in my sixteenth or seventeenth year, is a certainty, the memory of which has led the best of me to search for a means of finding it again on a long-term basis.

My childhood and adolescent memories are lined with a series of attempts to experience the beyond, and these haphazardly conducted attempts led me to the fundamental experience I'm speaking of. Around the age of six, no religious belief having been instilled in me, the problem of death presented itself in all its nudity. I spent horrible nights, clawed in the stomach and held in a stranglehold by the dread of nothingness, of "nothing left at all." One night, when I was about eleven, by relaxing my entire body I calmed my organism's revolt and terror before the unknown, and a new feeling was born in me: hope, and a foretaste of something imperishable. But I wanted more; I wanted a certainty. At the age of fifteen or sixteen, I began my experimental research, with no direction and somewhat at random. Finding no way to experiment directly with death—with *my* death—I tried to study my sleep, assuming an analogy between the two. I tried by various means to enter the state of sleep while remaining wide awake. This undertaking is less rigorously absurd than it seems, but it is dangerous in several respects. I could not pursue it very far: Nature gave me several serious warnings on the dangers I was courting. Still, one day I decided to confront the problem of death itself; I would put my body in as close a state as possible to physiological death, but would concentrate all my attention on staying awake and recording all that presented itself to me. I had some carbon tetrachloride on hand, which I used to kill the beetles I collected. Knowing that this product was in the same chemical order as chloroform, but more toxic, I thought I could regulate its action in a rather covenient way: the moment the blackout would occur, my hand would fall limp, taking with it the liquid-soaked handkerchief that I had been holding to my nostrils. Later, I repeated the experiment in the presence of comrades, who could have helped me if need be. The result was always the same—that is, it surpassed and staggered my expectations by shattering the limits of possibility and brutally throwing me into another world.

At first there were the ordinary phenomena of asphyxiation: pounding in the arteries, buzzing, jumping noises in the temples, painful repercussions of the slightest external noise, dancing lights; then the feeling that this was getting serious, that it was no longer a game, along with a rapid review of my life up to that point. If there was a slight anxiety, it was blended in with a bodily discomfort from which my intellect remained completely detached—the latter repeating to itself: "Careful, don't fall asleep, it's time to keep your eyes open." The phosphenes dancing before my eyes soon covered the whole space before me, filled by the noise of my blood. Noise and light filled the world and blended in a single rhythm. By then, I had already lost the use of speech, even internal speech; thought went much too fast to drag words along with it. In a flash, I noticed that I still had control over the hand holding the wad, that I heard words spoken near me, that I understood their meanings—but suddenly objects, words and meanings of words no longer had any significance. It was like those words which you have repeated for a long time, and which seem dead and foreign in your mouth: you still know what the word "table" means, you could use it correctly, but it no longer evokes its object in any way. Thus, all that was "the world" for me in my ordinary state was still there, but it was as if someone had emptied it of its substance; it was suddenly no more than a phantasmagoria, simultaneously empty, absurd, precise and necessary. And the "world" appeared in its unreality because I had suddenly entered another, intensely more real world, instantaneous and eternal, a blazing mass of reality and evidence in which I whirled around like a moth over a flame. At that moment I felt a *certainty,* and this is the point at which the spoken word must be satisfied with merely hovering around the facts.

Certainty about what? Words are heavy, words are slow, words are too soft or too hard. With these poor words, I can only emit imprecise propositions, whereas *my certainty* is, for me, the archetype of precision. All that I can still conceive and formulate of this experience in my ordinary state is this (but I would put my head on the block for it): I am certain of the existence of *something else,* of a *beyond,* of another world or of another kind of knowledge. And at that moment, I directly knew, I experienced that beyond in its very reality. It is important to repeat that, in this new state, I perceived and understood perfectly my ordinary state, the latter being contained in the former, as waking contains the dream and not inversely. This irreversible relation proves the superiority (on the scale of reality, or of consciousness) of the first state over the second.* I clearly thought: soon I will return to what they call my "normal state," and perhaps the memory of this appalling revelation will darken, but it is at this moment that I see the truth. I thought this without words, along with a superior thought which flashed through me—which thought *itself,* so to speak, in my very substance, at a speed tending toward instantaneousness. I was caught in the trap for all eternity, rushed headlong toward an always-imminent annihilation, across the terrifying mechanism of the Law that annulled me. "It's *that!* So it's *that!*"—such was the cry of my thought. Under pain of *worse,* I had to *follow* the movement; it was a terrible and increasingly difficult effort, but *I was forced* to make it—until the moment when, letting go, I no doubt fell into a brief state of blackout. My hand dropped the wad, I breathed air, and for the rest of the day I remained stunned, dazed, with a violent headache.

I will now try to define the inexpressible *certainty* by means of images and concepts. We must first understand that, with respect to ordinary thought, this certainty is at *a higher level of meaning.* We are accustomed to using images in order to signify concepts: for example, the image of a circle to signify the concept of circle. Here, the concept itself is no longer the final term, the thing to be signified. The concept—the *idea,* in the ordinary meaning of the word—is itself a sign of something greater. I remember that at the moment *the certainty* revealed itself, my

*The published French text mistakenly reads: "...proves the superiority of the second state over the first."

ordinary intellectual mechanisms continued to function; images were formed, concepts and judgments were thought, but without having to be encumbered by words, which gave these processes the speed and simultaneity they often have in moments of great danger—such as during a fall in mountain climbing.

The images and concepts I am going to describe were thus present at the moment of the experience, at a level of reality midway between the appearance of the daily "external world" and *the certainty* itself. However, some of these images and concepts are the result of subsequent invention, due to the fact that as soon as I wanted to relate the experience—first of all to myself—I was forced to use words, thus to make manifest certain implicit aspects of the images and concepts.

I will begin with the images, although images and concepts were simultaneous. They are visual and sonorous. They first appeared as a veil of phosphenes, more real than the "world" of the ordinary state, which I continued to perceive through them. A half-red and half-black circle was inscribed in a half-black, half-red triangle, the red half-circle being in the black half-triangle and vice versa. And all of space was indefinitely divided this way into circles and triangles inscribed one in the other, ordering and moving, becoming one another in a geometrically impossible way—that is, a way not representable in the ordinary state. A sound accompanied this luminous movement, and I suddenly realized that it was I who produced this sound. I was almost the sound itself; I maintained my existence by emitting this sound. The sound was expressed by a phrase that I had to repeat faster and faster, in order to "follow the movement." This phrase (I'm relating the facts without trying to disguise their absurdity) was pronounced something like: "Tem gwef tem gwef dr rr rr," with a tonic accent on the second "gwef"; and the last syllable, blending in with the first, gave a perpetual momentum to the rhythm which was, I repeat, that of my own existence. I knew that as soon as it went too fast for me to follow, the unnameable and appalling thing would happen. It was, in fact, always *infinitely close* to happening, and at a certain point... I can say no more.

The concepts, for their part, revolved around a central idea of *identity*: everything became the same at every instant. They were expressed in spatial, temporal and numerical schemas—

166

schemas present at that moment, but whose differentiation into these various categories and their verbal expression come, of course, after the fact.

The *space* in which these representations took place was not Euclidean, for it was a space such that any indefinite extension from a given starting point would return to this starting point. I believe this is what mathematicians call "curved space." Projected into a Euclidean plane, the movement could be described thus: an immense Circle, the circumference of which expands toward infinity, and which is perfect, pure and homogenous — *except for one point*. But because of this, the point expands into a circle which grows indefinitely, repels its circumference toward infinity and blends with the original circle, perfect, pure and homogenous — *except for one point*, which expands into a circle... And so on, endlessly and, to tell the truth, simultaneously; for at every instant the circumference expanding toward infinity reappears as a *point*. Not a central point — *that would be too easy* — but an eccentric point, which represents both the nothingness of my existence and the imbalance that this existence, by its specificty, introduces into the immense circle of Everything, which constantly *annuls me* by regaining its integrity (which it has never lost: I am the one who is always *lost*).

It is a perfectly analogous schema for *time*. This movement of indefinite expansion returning to its origin applies to duration (a "curved" duration) as well as to space: the last moment is perpetually identical to the first, all of it vibrates simultaneously, and it is only by necessity of representing things in our ordinary "time" that I must speak of an indefinite *repetition*. I saw what I have always seen, what I always will see, again and again, everything beginning anew at every instant — as if my specific and rigorously useless existence were, in the homogenous substance of the Never-changing, the cause of a cancerous proliferation of moments.

As for *numbers*, in the same way, the infinite multiplication of points, circles and triangles instantaneously culminates in regenerated Unity, perfect *except for me*. And this *except for me*, unbalancing the unity of Everything, engenders an indefinite and instantaneous multiplication which will immediately become mixed up with the limit, the regenerated unity, perfect *except for me*... And it all begins anew — always in the same place and instant, without the Everything being truly altered.

I would be led to the same absurd expressions if I kept trying to enclose the *certainty* in a series of logical categories. In the category of *causality*, for example, cause and effect are continuously enveloped and developed, passing one into the other because of the imbalance that is produced in their substantial identity by the emptiness, the infinitesimal hole that *I am*.

I have said enough for you to understand that the certainty I am talking about is simultaneously mathematical, experimental and emotional. *Mathematical* — or rather, *mathematical-logical* — which can be indirectly grasped through the conceptual description I have just tried to give, and which can be abstractly summarized: identity of the existence and non-existence of the finite in the infinite. *Experimental*, not only because it is founded on a direct vision (which would simply be observation, and not necessarily experimentation), not only because the experiment can be repeated at any moment, but because it was experienced at every instant in my struggle to "follow the movement" that annulled me, by repeating the phrase through which I pronounced myself. *Emotional* because — and this is the center of the experiment — *all of this is about me:* I saw my nothingness, or rather my perpetual annihilation, face to face, at every instant — *total* but not *absolute* annihilation. Mathematicians will understand me if I say "asymptotic."

I stress the certainty's threefold nature in order to prevent three types of misunderstanding on the part of the reader. First, I wish to spare unclear minds the illusion of understanding me, where, in answer to my mathematical certainty, they would have but vague sentiments about a mystery of the beyond, etc. Second, I wish to prevent psychologists, and especially psychiatrists, from taking my testimony not as a testimony, but as a psychological manifestation which is interesting to study and explainable by what they believe to be their "psychological science." It is to render their attempts vain that I have stressed the experimental (and not simply introspective) nature of my certainty. Finally, the very heart of this certainty, the cry: "That's me! All of this is about me!" should serve to discourage the curious who would want, in one way or another, to perform the same experiment. I warn them that it is a terrible experience, and if they want details about the dangers, they can ask me for them in private. I do not mean the physiological dangers (which are very great); for if, in return for the acceptance of serious illnesses or disabilities, or of a very perceptible abbreviation of the physical life-span, we could acquire *one* certainty, it would not be too high a price to pay. Nor do I only mean the very real risk of madness or permanent mindlessness, from which I escaped only by a piece of extraordinary luck which I cannot speak of in writing. The danger is much more serious, and the story of Bluebeard's wife illustrates it well: she opens the door to the forbidden closet, and the horrible sight that greets her will mark her as if with a red-hot iron in her innermost reaches. After the first experiment, furthermore, I spent several days in a state of "detachment" from what one usually calls the "real". Everything seemed an absurd phantasmagoria, no logic could convince me of anything whatsoever, and, like a leaf in the wind, I was ready to follow any external or internal impulse—which very nearly led me to commit several irrevocable "acts" (if I can use the word), nothing having any importance for me anymore. I repeated the experiment several times, always with exactly the same results. Or rather, it was always the *same* moment, the same instant that I found again and again, eternally coexistent with the illusory unfolding of my duration. Having seen the danger, however, I stopped renewing the experiment. And yet one day several years later, for a minor operation, I was anaesthetized with nitrous oxide: it was exactly the same thing, the same unique instant that I experienced—this time, it is true, all the way to total blackout.

My certainty, of course, had no need of external confirmation; rather, it was this certainty which suddenly awakened my senses to all kinds of stories that others have tried to tell of the same revelation. And in fact, I soon knew that I was not the only one, that I was not an isolated pathological case in the cosmos. First, several of my friends tried to undergo the same experience. For most of them nothing happened, save the usual phenomena that precede narcosis. Two of them went a bit further, but brought back from their excursions only vague images of profound stupefaction. One said that it was like the advertising posters for a certain cocktail, in which two café waiters are carrying bottles on the labels of which two café waiters are carrying bottles on the labels of which...; and the other, painfully racking his memory, tried to explain to me: "Ixian, ixan, i... Ixian, ixian, i...," which obviously translated into his language my "Tem gwef tem gwef dr rr rr..." But a third knew exactly the same reality as I, and we only needed exchange a glance to know that we had seen the same thing. It was Roger Gilbert-Lecomte—with whom I was to edit the review *Le Grand Jeu*—whose tone of profound conviction was but the reflection of our common certainty. And I am persuaded that this experience determined his life as it determined mine, albeit in a different direction.

Little by little, I discovered accounts of the same experience in my readings, for now I had the key to these narratives and these descriptions, whose relation to a same and unique reality I could not have suspected beforehand. William James speaks of the same thing. O. V. de L. Milosz, in his *Epistle to Storge*, relates it in a way that overwhelmed me by the terms he uses, terms which I found in my own mouth. The famous circle which was spoken of by a medieval monk, and which Pascal saw (but who saw and spoke of it first?), stopped being a cold allegory for me, and I knew that it was an all-consuming vision of what I had seen as well. And beyond all these more or less complete, human accounts (there was hardly a great poet in whom I didn't find at least a fragment of it), the confessions of the great mystics and—going still further—certain sacred texts of various religions brought me confirmation of the same reality: sometimes in its terrifying form, when perceived by a limited individual who had not made himself capable of receiving it—who, like me, tried to see infinity through the key-hole and found himself before Bluebeard's closet; sometimes in its peaceful form, blissful and intensely luminous, which is the vision of those who have really transformed themselves and can see this reality face-to-face without being destroyed by it. I am thinking, for example, of the revelation of Divine Being in the *Bhagavad Gītā*, of Ezekiel's visions and those of Saint John the Divine in Patmos, of certain descriptions in the *Tibetan Book of the Dead (Bardo Thödol)*, of a passage from the *Lankāvatāra Sūtra*...

Not having immediately and definitively gone mad, I gradually began to philosophize on the memory of this experience.

170

And I would have foundered in my own philosophy if someone had not happened along my path at the right moment to tell me, "Look, there is an open door: narrow and difficult of access, but a door nonetheless, and it is the only one for you."

(1943.)

BIBLIOGRAPHY

THE ABSURD EVIDENCE

"Freedom Without Hope": *Le Grand Jeu*, no. 1, summer 1928; pp. 19-25.

"Draft of an Introduction to the *Grand Jeu*": [first published in *L'Herne*, no. 10, November 1968; pp. 17-18].

"Introduction to the *Grand Jeu*": pamphlet, 1928.

"The 'Soul' of the Primitive": *Le Grand Jeu*, no. 1, summer 1928; pp. 48-49.

"More on the Books of René Guenon": no. 2, spring 1929, pp. 73-74.

"Pataphysics and the Revelation of Laughter": *Bifur*, no. 2, 25 July 1929; pp. 59-68.

"Nadja": *Les Cahiers du Sud*, no. 106, November 1928; pp. 317-321.

"On the Attitude of Criticism With Respect to Poetry": *Les Cahiers du Sud* (special issue: "Poetry and Criticism"), December 1929; pp. 80-91.

"Nerval the Nyctalope": *Le Grand Jeu*, no. 3, fall 1930; pp. 20-31.

"Open Letter to André Breton": *Le Grand Jeu*, no. 3, fall 1930; pp. 76-83.

"Surrealism and the *Grand Jeu*": [scheduled for inclusion in *Le Grand Jeu*, no. 4, fall 1932 (unpublished); proof pp. 11-12].

Lautréamont and the Critics": *La Nouvelle Revue Française*, no. 206, 1 November 1930; pp. 738-745.

"Asphyxiation and Absurd Evidence": [scheduled for inclusion in *Le Grand Jeu*, no. 4, fall 1932 (unpublished); proof pp. 1-5].

"The Role of Movement in the Complete Education of Man": *Régénération*, no. 54, October 1934 (pp. 28-30) and no. 55, November 1934 (pp. 14-17).

POWERS OF THE WORD

"The Limits of Philosophical Language"; *Recherches Philosophiques*, vol. IV. 1934-1935; pp. 209-231.

"On the Life of Basiles": *Mesures*, no. 3, 15 July 1935, pp. 39-56.

"Between Two Stools": *La Nouvelle Revue Française*, no. 275, 1 August 1936, pp. 413-415.

"The Powers of the Word in Hindu Poetics": *Mesures*, no. 2, 15 April 1938, pp. 79-106.

"Some French Poets of the 25th Century": *Fontaine*, no. 14, June 1941, pp. 338-344.

"Poetry Black, Poetry White": *Fontaine*, no. 19-20, March-April 1942, pp. 168-172.

"The Message of the *Bhagavad Gita*": *Les Cahiers du Sud*, no. 241, December 1941, pp. 669-671.

"The Determining Memory": [unpublished].

CITY LIGHTS PUBLICATIONS

Ginsberg, Allen. PLUTONIAN ODE
Goethe, J. W. von. TALES FOR TRANSFORMATION
Hayton-Keeva, Sally, ed. VALIANT WOMEN IN WAR AND EXILE
Herron, Don. THE DASHIELL HAMMETT TOUR: A Guidebook
Herron, Don. THE LITERARY WORLD OF SAN FRANCISCO
Higman, Perry, transl. LOVE POEMS FROM SPAIN AND SPANISH AMERICA
Jaffe, Harold. EROS: Anti-Eros
Jenkins, Edith. AGAINST A FIELD SINISTER
Kerouac, Jack. BOOK OF DREAMS
Kerouac, Jack. SCATTERED POEMS
Lacarrière, Jacques. THE GNOSTICS
La Duke, Betty. COMPANERAS: Women, Art & Social Change in Latin America
La Loca. ADVENTURES ON THE ISLE OF ADOLESCENCE
Lamantia, Philip. MEADOWLARK WEST
Lamantia, Philip. BECOMING VISIBLE
Laughlin, James. THE MASTER OF THOSE WHO KNOW
Laughlin, James. SELECTED POEMS: 1935-1985
Le Brun, Annie. SADE: On the Brink of the Abyss
Lowry, Malcolm. SELECTED POEMS
Marcelin, Philippe-Thoby. THE BEAST OF THE HAITIAN HILLS
Masereel, Frans. PASSIONATE JOURNEY
Mayakovsky, Vladimir. LISTEN! EARLY POEMS
Mrabet, Mohammed. THE BOY WHO SET THE FIRE
Mrabet, Mohammed. THE LEMON
Mrabet, Mohammed. LOVE WITH A FEW HAIRS
Mrabet, Mohammed. M'HASHISH
Murguia, A. & B. Paschke, eds. VOLCAN: Poems from Central America
Paschke, B. & D. Volpendesta, eds. CLAMOR OF INNOCENCE
Pessoa, Fernando. ALWAYS ASTONISHED
Peters, Nancy J., ed. WAR AFTER WAR (City Lights Review)
Pasolini, Pier Paolo. ROMAN POEMS
Poe, Edgar Allan. THE UNKNOWN POE
Porta, Antonio. KISSES FROM ANOTHER DREAM
Purdy, James. THE CANDLES OF YOUR EYES
Purdy, James. IN A SHALLOW GRAVE
Purdy, James. GARMENTS THE LIVING WEAR
Prévert, Jacques. PAROLES
Rey-Rosa, Rodrigo. THE BEGGAR'S KNIFE
Rigaud, Milo. SECRETS OF VOODOO
Saadawi El, Nawal. MEMOIRS OF A WOMAN DOCTOR
Sawyer-Lauçanno, Christopher, transl. THE DESTRUCTION OF THE JAGUAR
Sclauzero, Mariarosa. MARLENE
Serge, Victor. RESISTANCE
Shepard, Sam. MOTEL CHRONICLES
Shepard, Sam. FOOL FOR LOVE & THE SAD LAMENT OF PECOS BILL
Smith, Michael. IT A COME
Snyder, Gary. THE OLD WAYS
Solnit, Rebecca. SECRET EXHIBITION: Six California Artists of the Cold War Era
Solomon, Carl. MISHAPS PERHAPS
Sussler, Betsy, ed. BOMB: INTERVIEWS
Turyn, Anne, ed. TOP TOP STORIES
Tutuola, Amos. FEATHER WOMAN OF THE JUNGLE
Tutuola, Amos. SIMBI & THE SATYR OF THE DARK JUNGLE
Valaoritis, Nanos. MY AFTERLIFE GUARANTEED
Wilson, Colin. POETRY AND MYSTICISM